Lord of the Flies

WILLIAM GOLDING

Oxford
Literature
Companions

Notes and activities: Alison Smith
Series consultant: Peter Buckroyd

Contents

Introduction	4

Plot and Structure	6

Plot	6
Structure	26
• Timeline and setting	27
• Tragedy	28

Context	30

Biography of William Golding	30
Historical and cultural context of the novel	30
• World War Two	30
• Class and education	33
• Britishness	35
• Literary context	36

Characters	38

Main characters	38
• Ralph	38
• Jack	41
• Piggy	43
• Simon	45
• Roger	48
Minor characters	50
• Samneric	50
• The littluns	50
• The naval officer	50
• The parachutist	51
Character map	53

Language   54

Perspectives   54
Voices   56
Naming   57
Creating atmosphere   58
- Personification   58
- Pathetic fallacy   60
- Animalistic imagery   61
- Juxtaposition   62

Themes   64

Civilization and savagery   64
- Clothing   66
- Symbolism   68
- Games   69
Power and leadership   71
- Fear   72
Connecting themes   74

Skills and Practice   76

Exam skills   76
- Understanding the question   76
- Planning your answer   78
- Writing your answer   80
- What not to do in an exam answer   82
Sample questions   83
Sample answers   87

Glossary   95

Introduction

What are Oxford Literature Companions?

Oxford Literature Companions is a series designed to provide you with comprehensive support for popular set texts. You can use the Companion alongside your novel, using relevant sections during your studies or using the book as a whole for revision.

Each Companion includes detailed guidance and practical activities on:

- Plot and Structure
- Context
- Characters
- Language
- Themes
- Skills and Practice

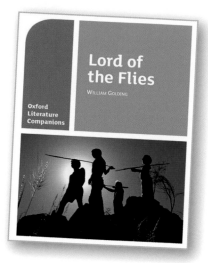

How does this book help with exam preparation?

As well as providing guidance on key areas of the novel, throughout this book you will also find 'Upgrade' features. These are tips to help with your exam preparation and performance.

In addition, in the extensive **Skills and Practice** chapter, the **Exam skills** section provides detailed guidance on areas such as how to prepare for the exam, understanding the question, planning your response and hints for what to do (or not do) in the exam.

In the **Skills and Practice** chapter there is also a bank of **Sample questions** and **Sample answers**. The **Sample answers** are marked and include annotations and a summative comment.

How does this book help with terminology?

Throughout the book, key terms are **highlighted** in the text and explained on the same page. There is also a detailed **Glossary** at the end of the book that explains, in the context of the novel, all the relevant terms highlighted in this book.

How does this book work?

Each book in the Oxford Literature Companions series follows the same approach and includes the following features:

- **Key quotations** from the novel
- **Key terms** explained on the page and linked to a complete glossary at the end of the book
- **Activity boxes** to help improve your understanding of the novel
- **Upgrade** tips to help prepare you for your assessment

To help illustrate the features in this book, here are two annotated pages taken from this Oxford Literature Companion:

Key quotations from the novel

Key terms explained on the page and at the end of the book

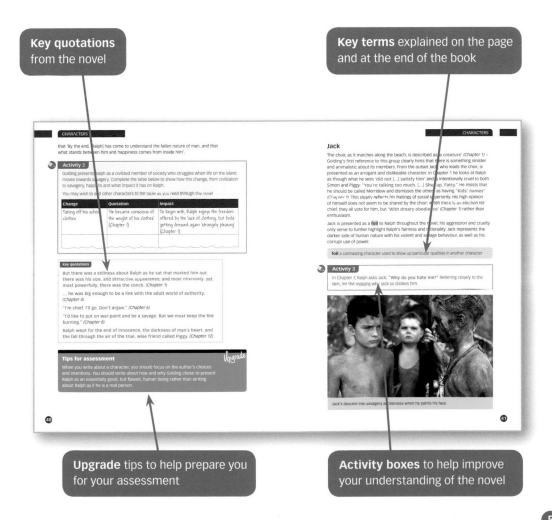

Upgrade tips to help prepare you for your assessment

Activity boxes to help improve your understanding of the novel

Plot

Chapter 1: The Sound of the Shell

The novel opens with a boy (who is later introduced as Ralph) appearing from the jungle and heading for the lagoon. He is soon joined by Piggy.

Ralph finds the conch shell, but it is Piggy who knows what it is and how to use it: **"We can use this to call the others"**. When Ralph blows it, other boys start to appear from the jungle. Piggy tries to find out who they all are. The last group to arrive is Jack and the choir who are described as **'a party of boys, marching approximately in step in two parallel lines and dressed in strangely eccentric clothing'**. Ralph betrays Piggy's trust by telling the others his nickname. Jack tries to assert his authority but there is an election to decide who is to be chief: Ralph is elected.

Jack, Ralph and Simon go to explore the island leaving Piggy to organize the other boys. They are excited by what they find. When they find a piglet, Jack wants to kill it but cannot bring himself to do so because **'of the enormity of the knife descending and cutting into living flesh'**.

- We discover a limited amount of information about how the boys came to be on the island, including a suggestion that their evacuation is due to a nuclear bomb threat.

- Hints are given about the boys' personalities through their behaviour and the way they speak to one another.

- Jack's comments about killing the pig **foreshadow** events later in the novel.

Although Ralph finds the conch shell it is Piggy who realizes its value in calling the boys together (seen here in the 1990 film)

Key quotations

"No grown-ups!"

Here at last was the imagined but never fully realized place leaping into real life.

Eyes shining, mouths open, triumphant, they savoured the right of domination.

[...]

Ralph spread his arms.

"All ours."

Activity 1

1. Read the extract below.

> **Key quotations**
>
> The shore was fledged with palm trees. These stood or leaned or reclined against the light and their green feathers were a hundred feet up in the air. The ground beneath them was a bank covered with coarse grass, torn everywhere by the upheavals of fallen trees, scattered with decaying coco-nuts and palm saplings. Behind this was the darkness of the forest proper and the open space of the scar.

    a) What is your first impression of the island from this description?

    b) Make two lists: one list of all the words with positive **connotations** in this extract and another list of all the words with negative connotations.

    c) Look closely at the third sentence. Why do you think that Golding chose to write about **'coarse grass'** and **'decaying coco-nuts'**? What is he trying to suggest about the island?

2. Now look at some of the other passages about the island in this chapter. Focus closely on the language that Golding uses. Write a paragraph which answers the following question: How does Golding present the island in Chapter 1 of *Lord of the Flies*?

3. Find some other examples of descriptions of locations on the island throughout the novel. Make notes on the language choices made and consider how Golding uses setting in the novel to show that appearances can be deceptive.

> **connotation** an implied meaning, such as ideas or qualities suggested by a word
>
> **foreshadow** hints at future events

Chapter 2: Fire on the Mountain

The chapter opens with a meeting between the boys. Jack expresses a desire for an army **"for hunting. Hunting pigs –"**. Ralph suggests that they need to have rules on the island and that the conch should be used as a signal for a person to speak.

During the meeting, the smaller boys mention that they are scared of **"a beastie, a snake-thing"**. Ralph tries to reassure them that the beast does not exist. Jack claims that he would hunt it.

Ralph suggests building a fire to be used as a signal and they build one on the mountain top. They use Piggy's glasses to light it. While they are discussing the rules, the fire spreads out of control: **'Piggy glanced nervously into hell'**. As the fire burns, Piggy realizes that one of the little 'uns is missing.

- The choir is described as being **'noticeably less of a group'**.
- Jack agrees with the idea of introducing rules, but only because he likes the idea of punishments for those who break them. This helps to develop our understanding of his character.
- Piggy continues to show that he is the most practical member of the group.
- The theme of Britishness becomes evident: the boys suggest that being English means following a strict and disciplined behavioural code.
- The fire shows the power of nature over the boys. The boys think that they are in control, but the untamed fire demonstrates that they are not.

Key quotations

"This is our island. It's a good island. Until the grown-ups come to fetch us we'll have fun."

"We've got to have rules and obey them. After all, we're not savages. We're English; and the English are best at everything. So we've got to do the right things."

Chapter 3: Huts on the Beach

Time has passed. Jack is hunting and has taken off his uniform. Meanwhile, Roger and Simon are building huts on the beach. Ralph reveals that the other boys are **"hopeless. [...] They're off bathing, or eating, or playing"** and there is a suggestion that he is becoming annoyed with Jack's obsession with hunting. Jack and Ralph argue but come to an uneasy truce: **'They looked at each other, baffled, in love and hate.'**

Simon wanders away from the rest of the group and vanishes into the jungle. As the chapter closes, he is alone and peaceful.

- Simon's actions (helping the littluns find food) show that he is a thoughtful and kind character. This chapter also makes it clear that he is an outsider, perhaps even more so than Piggy.
- The group of boys has already started to divide into smaller groups, which hints at the instability of their self-created community.
- As a hunter, Jack has taken off his uniform and this further suggests that he is moving away from 'civilized' Britishness.

Key quotations

"They talk and scream. The littluns. Even some of the others. As if –"

"As if it wasn't a good island."

[Piggy] wanted to explain how people were never quite what you thought they were.

While Ralph, Roger and Simon build huts, Jack takes off his uniform in preparation for hunting

Chapter 4: Painted Faces and Long Hair

The chapter opens with descriptions of the pattern of the days on the island and descriptions of the small boys (who are 'known now by the generic title of "littluns"') and their daily routines. As the littluns are playing on the beach, Roger and Maurice arrive and disrupt their game. While Maurice seems to feel 'the unease of wrong-doing', Roger has no such worries. When the littluns disperse, he follows Henry and torments him by throwing coconuts. He doesn't hurt him but it is clear that Roger is enjoying what he is doing.

Meanwhile, Jack paints his face with a mask, "Like in the war", to make hunting the pigs easier. He and some others go off to hunt.

Ralph, Piggy, Simon and Maurice are in the bathing-pool when Ralph sees the smoke of a ship in the distance: 'the smoke of home'. It soon becomes apparent that their own fire has gone 'out, smokeless and dead', and they race up the mountain to try to relight it. By the time they get there, the ship has vanished.

From the top of the mountain, they see the hunters carrying something. The hunters are excited that they have finally killed a pig and all they can talk about is the thrill of the hunt and the "lashings of blood". Eventually, Ralph is able to tell them about the ship. Piggy is upset by the reaction of the hunters and loses his temper. Jack pushes him and his glasses are broken in the scuffle.

There is a brief tussle for power, which Ralph wins by standing his ground. A new fire is lit and the pig is cooked. Jack tries to enforce his power by refusing Piggy any meat but Simon offers his to Piggy. This angers Jack.

At the end of the chapter, as the hunters once again describe the hunt, Ralph calls a meeting.

- It is clear that the mask has greater significance than a simple physical disguise. Golding suggests that it releases Jack from human ideas of morality.
- There is evidence of a divide beginning to form, with the hunters looking to Jack for leadership.

Key quotations

… the northern European tradition of work, play, and food right through the day, made it impossible for them to adjust themselves wholly to this new rhythm [of life on the island].

Roger's arm was conditioned by a civilization that knew nothing of him and was in ruins.

The mask compelled them.

There was the brilliant world of hunting, tactics, fierce exhilaration, skill; and there was the world of longing and baffled common-sense.

Activity 2

He sees that he has changed dramatically so that he doesn't even recognize himself.

He is pleased by the change and sees that it holds opportunities for him.

He knelt, holding the shell of water. A rounded patch of sunlight fell on his face and a brightness appeared in the depths of the water. He looked in astonishment, no longer at himself but at an awesome stranger. He spilt the water and leapt to his feet, laughing excitedly. Beside the mere, his sinewy body held up a mask that drew their eyes and appalled them. He began to dance and his laughter became a bloodthirsty snarling. He capered towards Bill and the mask was a thing on its own, behind which Jack hid, liberated from shame and self-consciousness.

Suggests he's like an animal.

1. Read the passage above and consider how Golding presents Jack's transformation when he wears the mask. Identify other phrases that you might comment on and make notes on the effects they create.

2. Write a paragraph explaining your ideas. Remember to use evidence from the text to support your answer.

3. Look at the extract below. Why do you think Ralph suggests that he, Piggy and Samneric **"smarten up a bit"**? What does he hope to achieve by it?

Key quotations

"Supposing we go, looking like we used to, washed and hair brushed – after all we aren't savages really and being rescued isn't a game –" *(Chapter 11)*

4. Make notes on how Golding uses clothing and appearance in the novel as a whole. What links does he make between appearance and attitude?

Chapter 5: Beast from Water

At the start of the chapter, Ralph is alone on the beach. As he paces, he realizes that the situation on the island has become both serious and unpleasant. He recognizes that Piggy has brains and that he is not as clever: **'Piggy, for all his ludicrous body, had brains.'**

At the assembly, Ralph sets out the problems as he sees them. He is very clear about his expectations of the other boys: **"You voted me for chief. Now you do what I say."** One of the littluns describes seeing the beast and it is revealed that Simon has been wandering around the island at night. Percival says that he has seen the beast coming out of the sea. Simon suggests that there is a beast but that **"maybe it's only us"**; the others dismiss this idea.

Ralph tries to get the meeting back on track but Piggy loses his temper again. Jack accuses Ralph of favouring Piggy and they argue. Jack and most of the other boys run off, leaving the assembly **'shredded'**. Ralph, Piggy and Simon are left behind.

Ralph is afraid of the way in which life on the island is falling apart and suggests that he should give up being chief. Simon and Piggy convince him that this is not in the best interests of the boys, stating that Jack **'can't hurt you: but if you stand out of the way he'd hurt the next thing'**.

- The importance of the conch is developed. Ralph relies on it as a symbol of authority, but Jack disrespects it. This helps to emphasize the difference in the characters.
- Ralph's decision not to blow the conch, because of his fear that the others might not return, suggests that some of the boys are no longer interested in **democratic** life on the island.
- Simon's suggestion that the beast is **"only us"** shows not only that he is the most self-aware of the boys but also suggests that the boys cannot escape the inherent fear on the island.
- Percival's recitation of his address, and later failure to do so, hints at the differences between the society they knew and the situation they are now in.

democratic a type of government which promotes social equality

Key quotations

[Ralph] found himself understanding the wearisomeness of this life, where every path was an improvisation and a considerable part of one's waking life was spent watching one's feet.

Ralph felt a kind of affectionate reverence for the conch.

"… maybe there is a beast […] maybe it's only us."

"What are we? Humans? Or animals? Or savages? What's grown-ups going to think?"

"Because the rules are the only thing we've got!"

"Bollocks to the rules!"

"If Jack was chief he'd have all hunting and no fire. We'd be here till we died."

Ralph still believes in democracy, represented by the conch

Activity 3

"Because the rules are the only thing we've got!"

1. Make a list of all the rules that the boys have created. Now divide the rules into groups. Can you see any patterns in the types of rules that they have suggested?

2. Do you agree with Ralph and Piggy that rules are important on the island? Explain why, with reference to the novel.

Chapter 6: Beast from Air

While the boys are sleeping, a parachutist lands on the mountain, dead.

In the morning, Sam and Eric go to tend the fire. Eric sees the body and the twins run back down the mountain. They wake Ralph and tell him that they have seen the beast. Ralph calls the boys together and Sam and Eric tell everyone what they have seen, although they are not very accurate in their description.

Jack decides that they are going to hunt the beast. In the ensuing argument, Jack says that they don't need the conch any more. Eventually, the boys decide where to look for the beast and it is Ralph who says **"We'd better take spears."**

When they arrive in the place where Jack thinks the beast is, he hesitates. It is Ralph who steps forward first: **"I'm chief. I'll go. Don't argue."** It soon becomes clear that there is no beast there and Jack joins Ralph. They decide that they need to go back up the mountain to where the twins saw the beast, but they know that the beast won't be there.

When Ralph wants to lead the boys to the top of the mountain, they are reluctant. They want to stay and **'roll rocks'**, but he insists that they do as they are told. It is Jack who leads them as they follow **'Mutinously'**.

- The battle going on above the island while the boys sleep is a reminder of the war from which they were evacuated. It reminds the reader that the grown-up world is no less hostile than life on the island.
- Simon is clear that he doesn't believe in the beast. He has always seen it as something human and he understands more about human nature than any of the other boys.
- Once more, Jack directly challenges Ralph's authority. The idea of using a rock as a weapon is also introduced by Jack.

Key quotations

Soon the darkness was full of claws, full of the awful unknown and menace.

"... we don't need the conch any more. We know who ought to say things."

However Simon thought of the beast, there rose before his inward sight the picture of a human at once heroic and sick.

Activity 4

1. Look at the extract below which describes the parachutist. What does Golding's description suggest about the reality of the 'beast'? Explain your ideas in detail with close reference to the text.

Key quotations

So the figure, with feet that dragged behind it, slid up the mountain. Yard by yard, puff by puff, the breeze hauled the figure through the blue flowers, over the boulders and red stones, till it lay huddled among the shattered rocks of the mountain-top. Here the breeze was fitful and allowed the strings of the parachute to tangle and festoon; and the figure sat, its helmeted head between its knees, held by a complication of lines. When the breeze blew the lines would strain taut and some accident of this pull lifted the head and chest upright so that the figure seemed to peer across the brow of the mountain. Then, each time the wind dropped, the lines would slacken and the figure bow forward again, sinking its head between its knees. So as the stars moved across the sky, the figure sat on the mountain-top and bowed and sank and bowed again.

---

2. Now look at the descriptions given of the beast by Sam and Eric at the beginning of Chapter 6. What do they say the beast looked like?

3. Why do you think their descriptions of the beast and the truth are so different? What possible reasons are there for them making up their descriptions?

4. Think about the other descriptions of the beast in the novel as a whole. What does the beast mean to each of the following:

- the littluns?
- Jack?
- Ralph and Piggy?
- Simon?

Tips for assessment

By now, you will probably know the plot really well. In your assessment, though, it's important that you don't just tell the story: the person marking your work will know it at least as well as you do!

Rather than telling the story, you need to be able to make links between the different parts of the novel, using quotations to support your ideas.

Chapter 7: Shadows and Tall Trees

At the beginning of the chapter, Ralph is following Jack along the **'pig-run'**. He contemplates his appearance and the changes that have taken place since they arrived on the island.

When they find a boar, Ralph throws his spear and hits it. He is pleased with the hunters' **'new respect'**, but Jack seems less impressed. The boys get carried away with re-enacting the hunt, at Jack's suggestion, and Robert is upset. Jack suggests that next time they should **"Use a littlun"** to make the re-enactment more real **'and everybody laughed'**.

The boys set off for the mountain top to find the beast, but Ralph soon realizes that they won't be back at the beach before dark. Simon offers to cut across the island to tell Piggy and the others. When they get to the bottom of the mountain, no one is brave enough to go up. Jack shames Ralph into going and Roger goes with them. At the top, Jack wanders off and finds **'a thing'**: the dead body of the parachutist. The boys are so terrified by what they see that **'presently the mountain was deserted, save for the three abandoned sticks and the thing that bowed'**.

- Simon reassures Ralph that **"You'll get back all right"**. This foreshadows later events: Simon does not survive to escape the island while Ralph does. Simon's insight is again suggested.
- Clear contrasts are drawn between life at home and life on the island.
- The re-enactment of the killing of the pig injures Robert and suggests that the boys are moving further away from 'civilization'. They seem less able to control their brutal urges.

> **Key quotations**
>
> Clothes [...] put on, not for decorum or comfort but out of custom.
>
> The desire to squeeze and hurt was overmastering.

Chapter 8: Gift for the Darkness

At the start of the chapter, Ralph, Piggy and Jack are discussing the beast. They are clearly afraid of it. Jack calls a meeting and tells the boys that Ralph thinks the hunters are cowards. He tries to encourage the boys to revolt against Ralph, but when that fails, shows his immaturity by saying **"I'm not going to play any longer"** and running off.

Left on the beach, Piggy is delighted that Jack has gone and barely conceals it. The boys agree that they can't return to the mountain and decide to move the fire to the beach instead. After their first attempt, they realize that some of the choir have disappeared. Piggy says that they are better off without them because **"It's them that haven't no common sense that make trouble on this island."** He and the twins collect fruit, and they sit down to eat a feast before realizing that Simon, too, has disappeared.

Along the beach, Jack tells the boys who were once the choir that he is going to be chief now. He sets out his plans to recruit more of the boys to his tribe and to kill another pig. He intends to **"leave some of the kill for [the beast]"**. They find and chase a sow until she is too tired to escape, then Roger and Jack kill her. The boys re-enact the kill before making a plan to raid Ralph's group to take fire from them. They put the sow's head on a stick as a gift for the beast.

On the beach, the fire is burning out. Ralph and Piggy discuss their situation and Ralph reveals that he feels helpless. Jack and two of the other boys, now described as savages, arrive and tell them about the feast. When they have gone, Ralph realizes that they have stolen fire.

The hunters come to steal fire to cook their meat, whereas Ralph understands that keeping it burning will attract rescuers

- Simon's conversation with the sow's head is clearly a result of his distressed mental state during his fit.
- The 'Lord of the Flies' reaffirms what Simon has already deduced, that the beast on the island is a reflection of the boys' own capacity for evil or inner darkness: **"You knew, didn't you? I'm part of you?"**
- It is significant that 'Lord of the Flies' is a literal translation of 'Beelzebub', another name for the devil.

> **Key quotations**
>
> "Sharpen a stick at both ends."
>
> "This head is for the beast. It's a gift."
>
> "The fire's the most important thing. Without the fire we can't be rescued. I'd like to put on war-paint and be a savage. But we must keep the fire burning."

Activity 5

1. Look closely at the description of Simon below. Think about how Golding presents Simon in this extract. What do you think Golding wants the reader to understand about Simon at this point?

> **Key quotations**
>
> Simon stayed where he was, a small brown image, concealed by the leaves. Even if he shut his eyes the sow's head still remained like an after-image. The half-shut eyes were dim with the infinite cynicism of adult life. They assured Simon that everything was a bad business. *(Chapter 8)*

2. Now think about Simon's role in the novel as a whole. Copy and complete the table below.

Chapter	Point	Evidence	What this suggests about Simon's role
1	Jack picks on Simon, which shows Jack's cruelty.		
		'Simon looked at them both, saying nothing but nodding till his black hair flopped backwards and forwards: his face was glowing.'	He is an observer. He notices things that other people don't and therefore understands more.
2	Simon shows kindness to Piggy and stands up to Jack.		

3. Use the evidence that you noted in the table to write an answer to the following question: What is Simon's role in the novel?

Chapter 9: A View to a Death

Simon awakens from his fit and makes his way back towards the beach past the corpse of the parachutist. Although he is sick at the terrible sight, he is able to work out what it is and untangles it. He then makes his way to the beach to tell the others.

On the beach, the boys are swimming. Piggy suggests that they should go to find Jack's group to **"make sure nothing happens"**. They can hear the hunters before they get to them: they seem to be having a feast. Eventually, Jack offers them a gift of meat. His authority is demonstrated by his throne and the way he orders the other boys around. Jack challenges Ralph's leadership directly by asking the boys whether they want to **"join my tribe and have fun"**. Piggy recognizes the danger and tries to get Ralph to leave as the storm breaks. Jack and the hunters begin to re-enact the pig hunt, and Ralph and Piggy feel compelled to join in.

As the dance reaches a **climax**, something crawls out of the forest and the boys circle round it. It is Simon, although the boys appear not to realize that it is him at first. He is **'crying out something about a dead man on a hill'**. Simon is killed: **'there were no words, and no movements but the tearing of teeth and claws'**. As the rain finally comes, the boys move away, leaving the body on the beach. The wind picks up and the parachutist is blown off the island and out to sea. At the end of the chapter, as the tide comes in, Simon's body is gently carried out to sea.

- **Pathetic fallacy** is used to reflect the building tension on the island.
- Simon's compassion once again shows itself in the freeing of the parachutist from **'the wind's indignity'**.
- Piggy shows a more forceful side to his character when he shouts at Ralph for the first time. This indicates how much he has been changed by the events.
- Ralph's natural power is suggested when the boys fall **'silent one by one'** following his arrival at Jack's camp.
- The boys' capacity for violence has extended to murder. It seems clear that they are aware that it is Simon they are attacking: **'Simon was crying out something about a dead man'**.
- The image of Simon at the end of the chapter being swept out to sea is **symbolic** of the end of civilization on the island.

> **climax** a high point; the most dramatic moment in a novel or play
>
> **pathetic fallacy** where something (like the building storm here) reflects the mood in a text
>
> **symbolic** using something to represent a concept, idea or theme in a novel

Key quotations

… he turned to the poor broken thing that sat stinking by his side. The beast was harmless and horrible.

Evening was come, not with calm beauty but with the threat of violence.

Piggy and Ralph […] found themselves eager to take a place in this demented but partly secure society. They were glad to touch the brown backs of the fence that hemmed in the terror and made it governable.

Tips for assessment

To reach the higher marks, it is important to think about the underlying meanings of the events and characters. For example, the conch, while being a useful object on the island, is deeply symbolic: it symbolizes democracy and order, and the boys' different responses to it tell the reader more about their attitudes.

There are plenty of other examples of symbolism in the novel: look for them carefully.

Chapter 10: The Shell and the Glasses

At the start of the chapter, Ralph is a changed figure: he is **'limping, dirty, with dead leaves hanging from his shock of yellow hair'**. Piggy reveals that there are no **'biguns'** left: they have all joined Jack's tribe. Ralph and Piggy discuss what they are going to do and Ralph laughs when Piggy suggests calling an assembly. They discuss the events of the night before and Ralph admits **"I'm frightened. Of us."** Piggy says that they must not tell Samneric that they were involved in Simon's death.

Roger joins the tribe at Jack's end of the island. He shows both his allegiance to Jack and his cruel side when he says that Jack is **"proper Chief"** because he has protected his area of the island with a weapon. It is revealed that Jack is punishing boys for no apparent reason.

At his meeting, Jack sets out his plans, which include watching out for the beast who he says **"came – disguised"**. One of the boys realizes that they have no means of making fire, so Jack says that they will go and take fire from Ralph's group.

On the beach, Ralph, Piggy and Samneric light a fire. As they prepare to sleep, the other boys attack the camp pretending to be the beast. They fight and all the boys are injured. Piggy's glasses are taken but the conch is left behind.

- Although it is not explicitly stated, it is clear that Samneric also saw what happened on the beach: **'The air was heavy with unspoken knowledge.'**
- Roger's admiration of the dangerously balanced rock hints at events yet to come.

- Jack is now referred to as Chief and seems to rule the tribe through fear and manipulation. Unlike Ralph, he does not consult the boys; he makes all of the decisions himself, acting more like a **dictator**.
- Piggy naively still views the conch as something of great significance.

dictator a person who has gained power by force and who has total power over a country

---

Key quotations

"What's the others going to think?"

"We got to forget this. We can't do no good thinking about it, see?"

"How could we – kill – it?"

He was a chief now in truth; and he made stabbing motions with his spear. From his left hand dangled Piggy's broken glasses.

The theft of Piggy's broken glasses is a key moment in the novel (seen here in the 1963 film)

Activity 6

Look at the extract below.

> **Key quotations**
>
> **At last Ralph cleared his throat and whispered something.**
>
> **Piggy whispered back.**
>
> **"What you say?"**
>
> **Ralph spoke up.**
>
> **"Simon."**
>
> **Piggy said nothing but nodded, solemnly.**

Then read the extract at the start of Chapter 10, which begins: **"That was Simon..."** and ends: **'There was loathing, and at the same time a kind of feverish excitement in his voice.'**

Make notes on how Golding uses language to reveal the boys' fears in these extracts. What does Golding reveal about how, if at all, they have changed during their time on the island?

Chapter 11: Castle Rock

Ralph tries to light the fire, but doesn't succeed. Piggy persuades him to blow the conch and call an assembly, but only a few littluns and Samneric come. Ralph suggests that they should approach Jack's tribe dressed in their old clothes to ask for fire. Samneric are worried because they know that Jack will be painted but Ralph says that they're not going to take spears.

When they set off, though, Ralph does have a spear and so do Samneric. Piggy struggles to see where he is going and is afraid. Roger stops them as they approach the tribe's camp and Ralph challenges him by blowing the conch to call an assembly. When Jack appears, it is clear that he is not interested in what Ralph has to say. Their verbal argument soon turns physical as Jack makes **'a rush and [stabs] at Ralph's chest with his spear'**. Piggy reminds Ralph of why they are there and Ralph tries to settle the issue with discussion.

Jack orders Samneric captured and then is **'inspired'** to cause further damage to Ralph's leadership. They start to fight again, but Piggy stops them. As he is speaking, Roger **'with a sense of delirious abandonment, leaned all his weight on the lever'** of the large rock and knocks Piggy into the sea. Within moments, **'the body of Piggy was gone'**. The conch is destroyed.

Jack seizes the opportunity to attack Ralph again and declares himself Chief. Ralph runs, leaving Samneric trapped by the tribe. Jack tries to force them to join the tribe but it is Roger who they respond to with **'quiet terror'**.

- Piggy suggests that they should wear their own clothes when they go to see Jack. He clearly still believes that there is hope that things can be fixed and that dressing in a more 'civilized' way might encourage more civilized behaviour.

- Roger's initial **'aiming to miss'**, which was foreshadowed in Chapter 4, turns into a deliberate act of violence.

- Piggy's death and the smashing of the conch are inextricably linked. The last symbols of order and civilization have been destroyed.

Key quotations

"Awful things has been done on this island."

"Supposing we go, looking like we used to, washed and hair brushed – after all we aren't savages really and being rescued isn't a game –"

Some source of power began to pulse in Roger's body.

... the conch exploded into a thousand white fragments and ceased to exist.

Jack isn't interested in talking, only in attacking Ralph

Activity 7

1. Look closely at the description of Piggy below. How does Golding present Piggy's character in this extract?

> **Key quotations**
>
> Piggy paused for a moment and peered round at the dim figures. The shape of the old assembly, trodden in the grass, listened to him.
>
> "I'm going to him with this conch in my hands. I'm going to hold it out. Look, I'm goin' to say, you're stronger than I am and you haven't got asthma. You can see, I'm goin' to say, and with both eyes. But I don't ask for my glasses back, not as a favour. I don't ask you to be a sport, I'll say, not because you're strong, but because what's right's right. Give me my glasses, I'm going to say – you got to!"
>
> Piggy ended, flushed and trembling. He pushed the conch quickly into Ralph's hands as though in a hurry to be rid of it and wiped the tears from his eyes.

2. Consider Piggy's role in the novel as a whole. Copy and complete the table below.

Chapter	Point	Evidence	What this suggests about Piggy's role
1	Piggy is intelligent and practical.	"I expect we'll want to know all their names," said the fat boy, "and make a list. We ought to have a meeting."	
2			
3			His glasses make him essential to island life.

3. Use the evidence that you noted in the table to write an answer to the following question: What is Piggy's role in the novel?

Chapter 12: Cry of the Hunters

Ralph hides in the bushes having escaped from Jack and the tribe. They keep watch for him. Ralph tries to convince himself that they will let him be an outlaw, but knows that 'These painted savages would go further and further'. As it gets dark, he returns to Castle Rock where he can hear the tribe's chant and sees Samneric. Although they are now part of the tribe, they explain that "– they made us. They hurt us –". Roger now appears to be Jack's right-hand man and it is him that Samneric are most afraid of: "You don't know Roger. He's a terror." Samneric reveal some of Jack's plans and Ralph hides again.

Ralph is hiding when he hears the savages calling out. Ralph feels fairly secure in the thicket where **'the great rock that had killed Piggy'** is now resting. He soon realizes that this is not the case when another rock is sent crashing nearby.

In panic, Ralph lashes out with his stick and wounds someone. The tribe then set fire to the thicket. Ralph finally realizes that there is no real chance of his survival: **'he would awaken with hands clawing at him; and the hunt would become a running down'**. He runs frantically across the island.

There is a naval officer on the beach and a boat behind. He has been drawn to the island by the smoke of the fire and asks what the boys have been doing. Ralph tells him that **"Only two [have been killed]. And they've gone"**. Ralph says that he is the boss. Jack begins to challenge this and then stops himself. The officer reacts to what Ralph tells him in an unemotional fashion, although he is **'a little embarrassed'**. He gives the boys time to **'pull themselves together'**, showing that he does not really understand what they have experienced.

Jack and his tribe are ready to attack and hunt Ralph down

- The covert in which Ralph hides reminds us of the places where the pigs hid earlier in the novel. Ralph has become the prey of the hunters and it seems inevitable that, like the pigs, he will eventually be killed too.

- The fire that is deliberately set reflects the accidental fire in Chapter 2 and it is clear that the tribe are hoping for a similar outcome. Golding repeatedly uses foreshadowing in the novel. It is **ironic**, however, that the fire at the end is started in order to kill Ralph, but the smoke that it causes results in all the boys being saved.

- Ralph's faith that the Navy will find them is proven correct, although it is now too late for the boy with the **'mulberry-coloured birthmark'**, Simon and Piggy.

- The tribe are now described as little boys again.

> **ironic** using irony; having the opposite effect to what was intended

Key quotations

… this was not Bill. This was a savage whose image refused to blend with that ancient picture of a boy in shorts and shirt.

Samneric were savages like the rest; Piggy was dead, and the conch smashed to powder.

Roger sharpened a stick at both ends.

He forgot his wounds, his hunger and thirst, and became fear; hopeless fear on flying feet.

For a moment he [Ralph] had a fleeting picture of the strange glamour that had once invested the beaches. But the island was scorched up like dead wood – Simon was dead – and Jack had… The tears began to flow and sobs shook him.

Activity 8

1. In this chapter, Golding's description of the boys changes from 'savages' to 'little boys' in a very short period. What does this suggest about the characters?

2. Now consider how the boys are referenced throughout the whole novel. Taking each chapter in turn, create a table which shows the different terms that Golding uses to describe the boys. One has been started for you below.

Chapter	Name	Who it describes
I	Choir	
I	Hunters	
4	Biguns	

3. Using the evidence you have gathered in your table, write an answer to the following question: How does Golding use different terms for the boys to reflect their changing attitudes and behaviour in the novel?

Structure

The novel begins and ends in the same place: on the beach. This is not an accident. Throughout the novel, Golding uses foreshadowing to draw the reader's attention to key ideas and themes, and to create a sense of **foreboding**.

> **foreboding** a feeling that something bad is going to happen

Examples of foreshadowing in the novel include:

- the accidental forest fire in Chapter 2 which foreshadows the deliberately started fire at the end of the novel
- the description of the choir boys as a **'creature'** in Chapter 1 which foreshadows Simon's realization that the beast is human in Chapter 5
- Roger's tormenting of Henry with rocks in Chapter 4 which foreshadows his murder of Piggy with the boulder in Chapter 11.

Activity 9

Tracing developments throughout the novel is one way to help you to improve your assessment mark.

1. Copy and complete the diagram below to show how the idea of the pig hunt develops throughout the novel and foreshadows the boys' decline.

> Jack wants to hunt the pig but isn't brave enough (Chapter 1)
>
> ↓
>
> "We're going to hunt pigs and get meat for everybody" (Chapter 2)
>
> ↓
>
> 'From the pig-run came the quick, hard patter of hoofs, a castanet sound, seductive, maddening—the promise of meat.' (Chapter 3)

2. Repeat this activity for each of the ideas listed below:

   a) the significance of the fire
   b) the presentation of the beast.

Tips for assessment

When you are writing about the structure of the novel, you won't get many marks for simply knowing when things happened. You need to try to say why Golding has structured the novel in this way. Think about what happens before and after major events. For example, the first time that Jack publicly refuses to follow the rules is in Chapter 5. This is the beginning of the breakdown of civilization which continues for the rest of the novel.

Timeline and setting

The timescale of the novel is deliberately made unclear. It is easy to see that some events happen in a few days, but others could be over much longer periods.

Activity 10

1. Copy and complete the table below to try to identify how time passes within the novel.

Chapter	Main events	Time	Evidence
1	The boys meet Ralph is made leader	On the first day	
2	The first mention of the beast The fire burns out of control	On the first day	
3		Several days later (maybe longer)	Jack has peeling sunburn
4			They have become used to the pattern of the day on the island.

2. Why do you think that Golding has chosen to make the timescale of the novel unclear? What effect does this have?

The island in the novel remains unnamed and the location is not specified, despite the description of the island itself being vivid.

In many ways the island could have been idyllic

Activity 11

1. Using the clues from the novel and a map, consider where in the world the island might be.

2. Why does Golding not make it clear where the island is located? Think about the limitations of specifying a location for the novel.

3. Would it have made a difference if the island was somewhere well known? Give reasons for your answer.

The description of the island develops as the novel progresses and Golding gives the reader more clues about the dual nature of the island. Although it appears beautiful on the surface, there is always an underlying sense of menace.

Tragedy

Traditionally, a tragedy is a text in which a high status character, such as a king, undergoes a change in fortune which leads to his downfall and death. In many ways, *Lord of the Flies* can be considered a tragedy because:

- Ralph is elected to be chief and therefore has high status.
- Jack takes control of the island which means that Ralph's fortune changes.
- Ralph is chased by the others who intend to kill him.

Tragedies usually follow a clearly defined structures, as shown opposite.

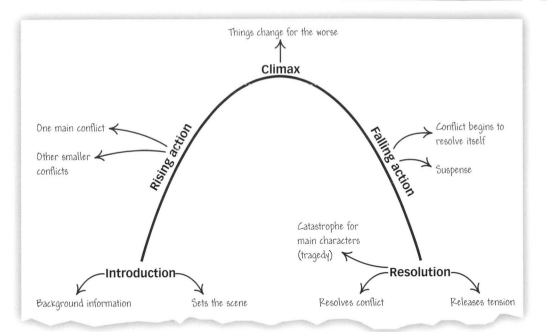

Things change for the worse

Climax

One main conflict ←

Other smaller conflicts ←

Rising action

Falling action

→ Conflict begins to resolve itself

→ Suspense

Catastrophe for main characters (tragedy) ←

—Introduction—

Background information   Sets the scene

—Resolution—

Resolves conflict   Releases tension

Activity 12

1. Look carefully at the structure of a tragedy given above. Copy the diagram and then add evidence from the text which suggests that *Lord of the Flies* follows the structure of a traditional tragedy.

2. In a tragedy, the main character dies. Thinking about *Lord of the Flies*, do you think it is a tragedy or not? Explain your ideas fully.

Writing about plot and structure

Upgrade

In your assessment, you will need to show that you appreciate how characters or ideas develop throughout the novel. You also need to show that you understand the key events and why they happen.

Make sure that you understand:

- how the plot develops, including how Golding has chosen to structure the novel
- how Golding has used the tragic structure to develop the narrative
- how Golding has used techniques such as foreshadowing to introduce ideas and create suspense.

Context

Biography of William Golding

- William Golding was born in Cornwall in 1911. After attending grammar school, he went to Oxford University where he studied English Literature.

- Following university, he trained as a teacher and taught at a boys' grammar school. His knowledge of boys and their behaviour is clearly evident in the novel.

- He joined the Navy in 1940 to fight in World War Two.

- After the war, Golding began writing *Lord of the Flies*. Its working title was *Strangers from Within*. His work was influenced by the events that he experienced during the war.

- *Lord of the Flies* was published in 1954 and is one of the most celebrated modern novels.

- In 1983, Golding was awarded the Nobel Prize for Literature.

William Golding (1911–1993)

Tips for assessment

You should only mention the author's background in relation to how it influences what Golding wrote in the text.

Historical and cultural context of the novel

World War Two

Golding wrote *Lord of the Flies* in the aftermath of World War Two (1939–1945). On one level, *Lord of the Flies* depicts a conflict between good and evil, between democratic leadership and **dictatorship**, similar to events in World War Two. Ralph represents **democracy** in the novel – he is elected chief by the other boys in a 'toy of voting' *(Chapter 1)* and uses the conch to ensure that all members of the society have their say. Jack, on the other hand, represents a dictatorship – he **usurps** Ralph's power, appointing himself "proper Chief" *(Chapter 10)* without consulting the other boys. As the democracy breaks down over the course of the novel, Jack is able to establish a dictatorial **regime**, based on fear of the beast and the boys' fear of his violent nature: "– they made us. They hurt us" *(Chapter 9)*. Golding appears to suggest that it can be difficult for people to resist this kind of leadership; this is evident both in the events of World War Two (especially Hitler's control over the German people) and in the power that Jack asserts in the novel.

Similarly, Golding uses *Lord of the Flies* to explore the idea that ordinary people can be persuaded to commit terrible acts of cruelty. This was something that he witnessed throughout World War Two. The events of the war changed Golding's view of the world and this is reflected in his portrayal of characters and events in the novel. Golding said:

> When I was young, before the war, I did have some airy-fairy views about man. [...] But I went through the war and that changed me. The war taught me different and a lot of others like me.

The atrocities of World War Two revealed a darker side to human nature: not only in the actions of Hitler, but also in the treatment of prisoners of war in Japanese camps and the **Allied** bombing of **civilians**. It was this human capacity for evil that interested Golding and inspired him to write *Lord of the Flies*. Golding demonstrated that during times of intense conflict the boundaries between right and wrong can become increasingly blurred. This is something that he clearly shows in the events of Chapters 9 and 10 as Piggy and Ralph join in with the dance that leads to Simon's murder and then try to deny their part in it.

Survivors of Nazi concentration camps were testimony to the atrocities that one group of humans can inflict on another

Allies the countries, including Britain, France and the United States, which combined forces to fight Nazi Germany

civilians the ordinary people who were not fighting in the war

democracy a system where everyone gets to vote for the leader and have a say in the way the country is run

dictatorship a system where the leader makes all of the decisions themselves; a dictator usually takes power by force and has not been elected

regime a system of government

usurp to take power illegally, often using force

Activity 1

Make a list of all of the events in the novel which suggest that 'normal' people can be influenced to commit terrible acts. Present your findings to the class.

In a lecture he gave in 1962, Golding claimed: 'People do not much like moral lessons. The pill has to be sugared, has to be witty or entertaining, or engaging in some way or other. […] It was this method of presenting the truth as I saw it in fable form which I adopted.' It is clear that this is what Golding aimed to achieve in the novel. The reader is engaged by the adventure, although they are at the same time shown the 'truth' as Golding saw it: that evil is **"part of you"** *(Chapter 8)*. He understood, as Simon does in the novel, that evil is not something that other people do, but that it is something that everyone is capable of.

Activity 2

1. Look at the extracts below. What do you think Golding wants the reader to understand about the boys' behaviour and attitudes at these points in the novel?

> **Key quotations**
>
> **Piggy and Ralph, under the threat of the sky, found themselves eager to take a place in this demented but partly secure society. They were glad to touch the brown backs of the fence that hemmed in the terror and made it governable.** *(Chapter 9)*
>
> **At once the crowd surged after it, poured down the rock, leapt on to the beast, screamed, struck, bit, tore. There were no words, and no movements but the tearing of teeth and claws.** *(Chapter 9)*
>
> **"You didn't see what they did –"**
> **"Look, Ralph. We got to forget this. We can't do no good thinking about it, see?"**
> **"I'm frightened. Of us. I want to go home. O God I want to go home."**
> **"It was an accident," said Piggy stubbornly, "and that's that."**
> **He touched Ralph's bare shoulder and Ralph shuddered at the human contact.**
> **[…]**
> **"… We was on the outside. We never done nothing, we never seen nothing."**
> *(Chapter 10)*

2. Using these extracts as a starting point, consider the novel as a whole. What do you think is Golding's message about war in *Lord of the Flies*? Explain your ideas with close reference to the text.

Class and education

The class system in Britain was still quite rigid at the time Golding was writing *Lord of the Flies*. While modern British society is not entirely classless, people were arguably more preoccupied with class and social status during the 1950s – an idea that is reflected in the relationships in the novel.

The class system in Britain in the 1950s consisted of three broad categories: upper class, middle class and working class. Upper-class people often came from very rich aristocratic families and inherited their wealth. Children of upper-class families would attend public, fee-paying schools. The middle classes (a much broader social group than the upper class) generally consisted of moderately wealthy people who worked in professional jobs or owned their own businesses. Middle-class children would attend either grammar schools or minor public schools. Working-class people were the poorest people in society and worked for a living, often in factories and shops.

Golding taught at grammar schools and was accustomed to the manners and behaviour of boys; something which is clear from the way in which the characters are portrayed within the novel. The manner in which they speak might seem odd to a modern reader, but they accurately reflect how boys of their age and class would have spoken at the time.

Activity 3

Look closely at the extract below. Using the annotations as a guide, make notes to show how Golding uses language to present the different social statuses of Piggy and Ralph.

What does Piggy's non-standard language imply about his social status in the novel?

"I can't swim. I wasn't allowed. My asthma –"

"Sucks to your ass-mar!"

Piggy bore this with a sort of humble patience.

"You can't half swim well."

Ralph paddled backwards down the slope, immersed his mouth and blew a jet of water into the air. Then he lifted his chin and spoke.

The boys refer to their fathers differently.

How does Ralph's use of language compare to Piggy's? What does it suggest?

"I could swim when I was five. Daddy taught me. He's a commander in the Navy. When he gets leave he'll come and rescue us. What's your father?"

Shows that judgements are made based on family background.

Piggy flushed suddenly.

The boys refer to their fathers differently.

"My dad's dead," he said quickly, "and my mum –"
(Chapter 1)

The boys are presented as being from different backgrounds; some of the boys may have attended public school, whereas others are likely to be grammar-school educated.

The upper classes

The language used by Jack in Chapter 1 suggests that he and the choir may have come from a public school; he uses Latin words such as 'matins' and 'precentor'. Parents would pay for their children to be educated at public schools and so students at these schools would often be from the wealthiest families in England. Their schooling would have been very formal and ordered, with masters and senior boys administering punishments to boys who did not follow the rules. Indeed, Jack seems to relish the opportunity to punish boys on the island who do not obey the group's

Many public school boys would have regarded themselves as superior to grammar school boys in the 1950s

instructions: '"We'll have rules!" he cried excitedly. "Lots of rules! Then when anyone breaks 'em –"' (Chapter 2).

Jack wants to be known as Merridew, which suggests that he sees himself as being superior to the other boys, who have "Kids' names" (Chapter 1). His treatment of Piggy, for example when he says "Shut up, Fatty" (Chapter 1), may also suggest that he thinks that it is acceptable to treat people of a lower social class in a discriminatory way.

The middle classes

The other boys appear to be middle class (and therefore potentially less wealthy): Ralph's father is in the Navy and Piggy's aunt runs a sweet shop. They would have attended either minor (less famous) public schools or grammar schools. Grammar schools were run along similar, although less regimented, lines but were free for children to attend. It is important to note, however, that there was still a degree of variation within the middle classes; for example, Piggy is presented as having a lower social standing than Ralph in the novel.

Activity 4

1. Find five examples from the novel which suggest that the boys have different educational and family backgrounds.

2. How does Golding present the different backgrounds of the boys in the novel? Think about how they speak to and behave with one another.

3. Now consider the following question: Does Golding suggest that one type of background is better than another in *Lord of the Flies*? What evidence do you have for this?

Tips for assessment

You should only write about the historical and cultural context of the novel where it is relevant to the exam question.

Britishness

Until the 1950s, Britain was in charge of a large **empire** of countries. There was a strong sense that being British meant being the **"best at everything"** *(Chapter 2)* and this is demonstrated in some of the boys' attitudes.

> **empire** a group of countries spread over a large area which is ruled by one person (e.g. Queen Victoria)

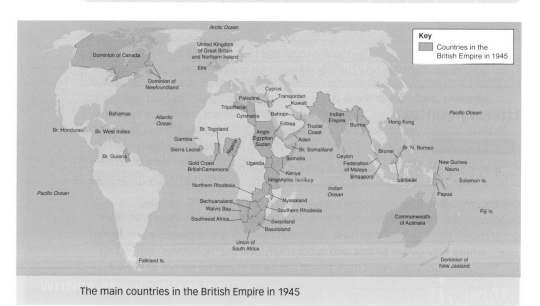

The main countries in the British Empire in 1945

Key quotations

"My father's in the Navy. He said there aren't any unknown islands left. He says the Queen has a big room full of maps and all the islands in the world are drawn there. So the Queen's got a picture of this island." *(Chapter 2)*

"I should have thought that a pack of British boys – you're all British aren't you? – would have been able to put up a better show than that" *(Chapter 12)*

Main characters

Ralph

'The boy with the fair hair' *(Chapter 1)* is the first character that we meet on the island. Described as having a 'mildness about his mouth and eyes that proclaimed no devil' *(Chapter 1)*, he is instantly likeable despite his later betrayal of Piggy's nickname to the others, which reveals his relative immaturity. Although he is one of the oldest boys on the island, he is rather childish in many ways. He calls his father Daddy and firmly believes that "he'll come and rescue us" *(Chapter 1)*. It is this naivety which is later responsible for his misplaced belief that Jack can be persuaded to do the right thing.

Ralph, a golden Adonis, in the 1963 film

Golding presents Ralph as an **Adonis-like** figure, with his 'golden body' *(Chapter 1)* and physical ability. It is no surprise that the other boys, especially Piggy, look up to him since he seems to embody the physical ideals of the period. While he is physically superior to the other boys, he is not as quick thinking or as knowledgeable as Piggy, a fact which he acknowledges several times over the course of the novel.

Adonis-like like a god

> **Key quotations**
>
> He was searching his mind for simple words so that even the littluns would understand what the assembly was about. Later perhaps, practised debaters – Jack, Maurice, Piggy – would use their whole art to twist the meeting... *(Chapter 5)*

The other boys recognize Ralph's leadership qualities from the outset: he does not put himself forward as chief but is elected nonetheless. As a leader, he is direct and clear: "We can't have everybody talking at once. We'll have to have 'Hands up' like at school" *(Chapter 2)*. His leadership is based on a democratic system; he allows all of the boys to have a say, even when doing so creates more problems than it solves, such as when the vote reinforces the fear of the beast rather than diminishing it. The conch is a key part of his leadership. It is what seals his election in the first place and he uses it to assert his authority: **'Ralph had to wave the conch once more'** *(Chapter 5)*. He takes his role seriously but does so with a quiet authority which is respected by the others. When the hunters let the fire go out, Ralph literally stands his ground and forces them to rebuild the fire **'three yards away and in a place not really as convenient'** *(Chapter 4)*. Unlike Jack, he does not resort to aggression and violence to get his way.

Ralph does find the role difficult, however: **'He found himself understanding the wearisomeness of this life, where every path was an improvisation and a considerable part of one's waking life was spent watching one's feet'** *(Chapter 5)*. He realizes that the role of a leader is to think, for which **'you had to be wise'** *(Chapter 5)* – this is not something that comes naturally to him. When they go to find the beast in Chapter 6, he is glad that Jack takes the lead and is **'thankful to have escaped responsibility for a time'** *(Chapter 6)*.

Activity 1

1. List all the qualities of a good leader. Does Ralph demonstrate those qualities? Find a range of examples from the text to support your points.

2. Now consider whether any of the other characters demonstrate these leadership qualities.

Although Ralph initially revels in the freedom offered by life on the island, he also retains a strong sense of his English identity. In Chapter 1, Golding describes how, for Ralph, putting **'on a grey shirt once more was strangely pleasing'**. Ralph clearly associates the clothes he wears with his identity. When he sets off on his ill-fated mission to persuade Jack to give back Piggy's glasses, he says that **"We'll wash"** […] **"We ought to comb our hair"** *(Chapter 11)* as if clothing is a kind of protection from the terrible things that have been happening. Throughout the novel, Ralph represents the 'civilized' world that the boys have left behind.

However, Golding also reveals a darker side to Ralph; this is something that Ralph does not always have full control of. When Jack mocks Piggy in Chapter 4, Ralph **'felt his lips twitch; he was angry for himself for giving way'**. This manifests itself again in Chapter 7, where the mock pig hunt spirals out of control and Robert is hurt. Ralph is caught up in the excitement and the **'over-mastering' 'desire to squeeze and hurt'** *(Chapter 7)*. This foreshadows Ralph's involvement in the murder of Simon in Chapter 9, which he describes with **'loathing, and at the same time a kind of feverish excitement in his voice'** *(Chapter 10)*. Ralph is clearly torn between two reactions to his behaviour: loathing and excitement.

At the end of the novel, Ralph is only saved by the unexpected arrival of the naval officer. By this time, the sense of society on which he based his leadership has long gone and there is no possibility of it being restored. Indeed the conch, the symbol of order, has **'exploded into a thousand white fragments and ceased to exist'** *(Chapter 11)*. In his famous essay on *Lord of the Flies*, 'Fable', Golding himself said that 'By the end, [Ralph] has come to understand the fallen nature of man, and that what stands between him and happiness comes from inside him'.

Activity 2

Golding presents Ralph as a civilized member of society who struggles when life on the island moves towards savagery. Complete the table below to show how this change, from civilization to savagery, happens and what impact it has on Ralph.

You may wish to add other characters to the table as you read through the novel.

Change	Quotation	Impact
Taking off his school clothes	'He became conscious of the weight of his clothes' (Chapter 1)	To begin with, Ralph enjoys the freedom offered by the lack of clothing, but finds getting dressed again 'strangely pleasing' (Chapter 1).

Key quotations

But there was a stillness about Ralph as he sat that marked him out: there was his size, and attractive appearance; and most obscurely, yet most powerfully, there was the conch. *(Chapter 1)*

… he was big enough to be a link with the adult world of authority. *(Chapter 4)*

"I'm chief. I'll go. Don't argue." *(Chapter 6)*

"I'd like to put on war-paint and be a savage. But we must keep the fire burning." *(Chapter 8)*

Ralph wept for the end of innocence, the darkness of man's heart, and the fall through the air of the true, wise friend called Piggy. *(Chapter 12)*

Tips for assessment

Upgrade

When you write about a character, you should focus on the author's choices and intentions. You should write about how and why Golding chose to present Ralph as an essentially good, but flawed, human being rather than writing about Ralph as if he is a real person.

Jack

The choir, as it marches along the beach, is described as **'a creature'** *(Chapter 1)* – Golding's first reference to this group clearly hints that there is something sinister and animalistic about its members. From the outset Jack, who leads the choir, is presented as an arrogant and dislikeable character. In Chapter 1 he looks at Ralph as though what he sees **'did not [...] satisfy him'** and is intentionally cruel to both Simon and Piggy: **"You're talking too much. [...] Shut up, Fatty."** He insists that he should be called Merridew and dismisses the others as having **"Kids' names"** *(Chapter 1)*. This clearly reflects his feelings of social superiority. His high opinion of himself does not seem to be shared by the choir: when there is an election for chief, they all vote for him, but **'With dreary obedience'** *(Chapter 1)* rather than enthusiasm.

Jack is presented as a **foil** to Ralph throughout the novel; his aggression and cruelty only serve to further highlight Ralph's fairness and rationality. Jack represents the darker side of human nature with his violent and savage behaviour, as well as his corrupt use of power.

> **foil** a contrasting character used to show up particular qualities in another character

Activity 3

In Chapter 7, Ralph asks Jack: **"Why do you hate me?"** Referring closely to the text, list the reasons why Jack so dislikes him.

Jack's descent into savagery accelerates when he paints his face

From the beginning of the novel, Jack shows that he has an aggressive nature: he wants the choir to be either an army or a group of hunters. Although his first attempt at hunting is unsuccessful, he works to perfect his skills. He says that he wants to be rescued too, but he soon loses interest and asserts that he'd "like to catch a pig first" *(Chapter 3)*. When he paints his face for the first time, he feels 'liberated from shame and self-consciousness' *(Chapter 4)* and this marks a change in his ability to hunt, as well as an increase in his violent behaviour. When, in Chapter 4, he finally kills a pig, he is proud and delighted, but also realizes 'the awful implications' of the fire going out. Despite his apparent bloodthirstiness, there is recognition that he is uncomfortable about the kill: 'He noticed blood on his hands and grimaced distastefully' *(Chapter 4)*.

Jack craves control. When Ralph is elected over him, 'He started up, then changed his mind and sat down again' *(Chapter 1)*. Later, when the boys don't support his take-over bid, he cries with humiliation before running away from the group. When he does form his own tribe, he becomes a self-appointed 'proper Chief' *(Chapter 9)* and rules through violence and fear. He relishes in punishing the boys without reason and covers his inadequacy with the red and white clay. Jack is a **megalomaniac** – he is obsessed with power and the material gains associated with it; he insists that the mountain "would make a wizard fort" *(Chapter 6)* and is described as being 'painted and garlanded [...] like an idol' *(Chapter 9)* in the midst of his newly formed tribe.

When the idea of the beast is first introduced, Jack is clear that it does not exist: "If there was a beast, I'd have seen it. [...] there is no beast in the forest" *(Chapter 5)*. Later, he claims: "If there's a beast, we'll hunt it down!" *(Chapter 5)* He is manipulative and realizes that he can use the threat of the beast as a means to control others. After Simon is apparently mistaken for the beast and killed, he says that "[The beast] came – disguised. He may come again" *(Chapter 5)* to ensure that the tribe continues to do as he wants.

Key quotations

[Jack has] uniformed superiority and offhand authority *(Chapter 1)*

"I ought to be chief [...] because I'm chapter chorister and head boy. I can sing C sharp." *(Chapter 1)*

They knew very well why he hadn't [killed the pig]: because of the enormity of the knife descending and cutting into living flesh; because of the unbearable blood. *(Chapter 1)*

For a minute [he] became less a hunter than a furtive thing, ape-like among the tangle of trees. *(Chapter 3)*

He tried to convey the compulsion to track down and kill that was swallowing him up. *(Chapter 3)*

Activity 4

1. Golding highlights the differences between Ralph and Jack in terms of their personalities and leadership styles. Complete the table below to show how Golding presents the differences between them.

Ralph	Jack
Described as 'golden', 'Adonis-like'	Described as 'black', 'ugly without silliness'
	Looks like he gets angry easily – 'turning, or ready to turn, to anger'

2. Although there are lots of differences between Jack and Ralph, Golding also hints at similarities in their behaviour and attitudes. Find five examples of similarities between Jack and Ralph, supporting your answers with references to the text.

3. Considering the ideas above, what do you think Golding is suggesting about the relationship between **anarchy** (represented by Jack) and **order** (represented by Ralph)?

> **anarchy** lawlessness
>
> **megalomaniac** a person obsessed with power
>
> **order** a state in which rules established to control the behaviour of a community are obeyed

Piggy

Piggy is probably the most likeable character in the novel, although he is largely overlooked by many of the other characters. It is Piggy who, despite his **"ass-mar"** *(Chapter 4)*, thick spectacles and 'ludicrous body' *(Chapter 5)*, is actually the most intelligent of the boys: his appearance leads the others to assume that he is 'an irrelevance' *(Chapter 1)*. Piggy realizes what the conch is and how to use it, although he mistakenly assumes that Ralph, too, knows how to blow it and that **"That's why [he] got the conch out of the water"** *(Chapter 1)*. Piggy is the most practical of all the boys: it is he who suggests that they should **"make a list. We ought to have a meeting"** *(Chapter 1)* and who suggests that they **"ought to have made [...] shelters"** *(Chapter 2)*. Piggy also becomes inadvertently essential to the survival of the boys, as his glasses provide the means for making fire. However, Piggy ultimately fails to recognize the important practical function that his glasses serve on the island. When the hunters attack Piggy and Ralph's camp, Piggy assumes that they will attempt to steal the conch and is confused when he realizes his glasses have gone. When Jack seizes the glasses, Piggy ceases to have a practical function in the novel and his death is therefore inevitable.

Activity 5

1. Make a list of all of the qualities that make Piggy a natural candidate for leadership. Then make a list of all of the reasons why the other boys don't consider him a leader.

2. Why do you think Golding gives Piggy these negative characteristics? What is he trying to say about human nature and how people judge one another?

Piggy is generally **pessimistic**: **"I've been watching the sea. There hasn't been a trace of a ship. Perhaps we'll never be rescued"** *(Chapter 2)*, but he is often right. When the forest catches fire in Chapter 2, it is Piggy who realizes that there is a boy missing, even though it is Ralph who tries to claim credit for the idea of making a list of names.

pessimistic naturally negative

He is fiercely loyal to Ralph, despite Ralph's early betrayal of his nickname and the fact that **'what intelligence had been shown was traceable to [himself]'** *(Chapter 1)*. He shows no resentment that his own contributions are either overlooked or credited to others. He still fiercely adheres to the social and moral codes of his previous life, showing great concern for what the **"grown-ups [are] going to say"** *(Chapter 5)*.

Despite this, he is involved in the killing of Simon. Unlike Ralph, he is unwilling to admit that he has a darker side and insists they do not talk about the incident in front of Samneric: **"It was an accident"** *(Chapter 10)*.

Even when Ralph is searching for a compromise with Jack, Piggy is able to see that it is a pointless task. He understands better and sooner than anyone else that Jack hates Ralph and that **"We're all drifting and things are going rotten"** *(Chapter 5)*. He is rightly afraid of Jack, although it is not Jack, in the end, who is directly responsible for his death. Although he is clearly intelligent and understands the motivations of others, even he fails to recognize the danger posed by Roger. It is significant that Piggy and the conch are destroyed simultaneously: they are both representative of the destruction of democracy and civilization.

Tips for assessment

Only mention the symbolic function of the characters if it is relevant to your exam question. You should always be selective in your answer, rather than telling the examiner everything you know about a character.

Activity 6

If Ralph represents fairness and democracy, and Jack represents the dark side of human nature, what do you think Piggy represents?

Look at the key quotations above and the other quotations about Piggy from this chapter. Then consider what you think Piggy's role in the novel is. Support your ideas with quotations from the text.

Simon's thoughtfulness and insight mark him as an outsider

Simon

Simon's introduction by Jack makes it clear from the outset that he is considered strange, even by those he attended school with. He is 'a skinny, vivid little boy, with a glance coming up from under a hut of straight hair' *(Chapter 1)*. He, like Piggy, is a thinker, but unlike Piggy, Simon is more respected by the other boys. However, his 'faints' mark him as an outsider.

He repays Ralph's decision to pick him for the first exploration of the island with loyalty, even though he is a chorister. He is practical, considerate and a diligent worker, helping with the construction of the shelters. When the question of the beast is introduced, it is Simon who demonstrates real insight by asserting that the beast is not a real thing but something within them all: **"maybe it's only us"** *(Chapter 5)*. He understands that people have a dark side and recognizes that the beast is simply a projection of the boys' fears and their own capacity for evil.

Simon continues to show a great deal of insight throughout the novel, seeing things that the other boys do not; for example, he recognizes the truth about the dead parachutist and he predicts that Ralph will escape. He represents the moral centre of the novel as he is the only one of the boys who does not give in to to the dark side of human nature.

When he finds the Lord of the Flies, he imagines that it is speaking to him and the warnings that he hears foreshadow later events. The pig's head predicts Simon's death by asserting: **"You know perfectly well you'll only meet me down there – so don't try to escape!"** *(Chapter 8)*. Following his fit and 'conversation' with the Lord of the Flies, he is the only one brave enough to get close to the beast and discovers that it is a **'poor broken thing'** *(Chapter 9)* – the dead parachutist. He shows his humanity by freeing it from the rocks.

Activity 7

1. Look for evidence from the novel that shows that:

    a) Simon is presented as loyal.

    b) Simon possesses an unusual insight into events on the island.

    c) Simon is presented as an outsider.

2. Why do you think Golding has chosen to present Simon in this way? Write a paragraph explaining your views and include quotations.

Simon is also clearly aligned to Christian ideals in the novel and Golding often alludes to this aspect of his character. In Chapter 3, the refuge that he seeks in the forest is likened to the Garden of Eden – it is a peaceful paradise that becomes corrupted by the **'obscene'** gift for the beast in Chapter 8. Similarly, in Chapter 8, Simon's conversation with the Lord of the Flies is reminiscent of Christ's confrontation of the devil during his 40-day fast. It could be argued that Simon is portrayed as a **martyr** who dies trying to deliver the truth about evil or sin to the boys. His death shows what the boys are truly capable of and marks a point of no return for them.

martyr someone who dies for their beliefs, normally religious

Activity 8

Make notes on other occasions in the novel when Golding draws parallels between Simon and Christian teachings. Make sure that you back up your ideas with evidence from the text.

Tips for assessment

When you are writing about character in your assessment, it is important to pay close attention to the language that Golding uses. Look at the annotated extract below for an example of how you can use analysis of small linguistic details to improve your answer.

It seems as though nature is in mourning for Simon.

Softly, surrounded by a fringe of inquisitive bright creatures, itself a silver shape beneath the steadfast constellations, Simon's dead body moved out towards the open sea. *(Chapter 9)*

Like a halo made of light, this supports the idea that Simon is associated with goodness or morality.

Suggests that Simon is now part of nature/the heavens; like the 'steadfast constellations', his body is a 'silver shape'.

Key quotations

[Simon had] eyes so bright they had deceived Ralph into thinking him delightfully gay and wicked. *(Chapter 3)*

Simon became inarticulate in his effort to express mankind's essential illness. *(Chapter 5)*

However Simon thought of the beast, there rose before his inward sight the picture of a human at once heroic and sick. *(Chapter 6)*

In Simon's right temple, a pulse began to beat on the brain. *(Chapter 8)*

Only the beast lay still, a few yards from the sea. Even in the rain they could see how small a beast it was; and already its blood was staining the sand. *(Chapter 9)*

Roger

Roger soon becomes a prominent and brutal member of the hunters

To begin with, Roger seems to be just another one of the boys. When the discussion about a leader takes place, it is Roger who suggests that they take a vote and thus he introduces the idea of democracy to the island. It is not until Chapter 4, however, that it becomes clear that he has an unpleasant side: he deliberately **'led the way straight through the [littluns'] castles, kicking them over, burying the flowers, scattering the chosen stones'**. He is presented as a bully, throwing stones at Henry; however, at this stage, still **'conditioned by […] civilization'** *(Chapter 4)*, Roger intentionally misses.

Later, he is eager to be close to the action in the mock hunt and offers to go to look for the beast with Ralph and Jack. When the pig is caught in Chapter 8, it is Roger who **'found a lodgment for his point and began to push till he was leaning with his whole weight'**. His method of killing is violent and cruel, and foreshadows his intended method of killing Ralph in the final chapter.

Roger cements his place in Jack's tribe with the killing of Piggy when **'with a sense of delirious abandonment, [he] leaned all his weight on the lever'** *(Chapter 11)*. He is immediately accepted as Jack's enforcer, having proven himself capable of extreme violence without guilt. The fact that he once again **'sharpened a stick at both ends'** *(Chapter 12)* shows the extent of his savagery: he intends to use the stick to mount Ralph's head in the same manner that he mounted the pig's head.

Activity 9

1. Look at Golding's description of Roger as he kills Piggy: **'with a sense of delirious abandonment, [he] leaned all his weight on the lever'** *(Chapter 11)*. What does this quotation add to the reader's understanding of his character?

2. Do you think that Roger is a truly evil character? Find as much evidence as you can which suggests that he has a good side as well as a bad side.

He is a potential rival for the leadership of the tribe since he is the one who the littluns are more scared of: **"You don't know Roger. He's a terror"** *(Chapter 12)*. He represents the capacity for evil that is present in everyone and suggests that, once social boundaries are removed, evil has the opportunity to flourish. Roger is undoubtedly the character who descends into the basest savagery in the novel; however, it is important to remember that Golding complicates the reader's view of his character as Roger is the one who initially introduces democracy to the island.

Key quotations

[He sat] assimilating the possibilities of irresponsible authority. *(Chapter 10)*

The hangman's horror clung to him. *(Chapter 11)*

Roger advanced upon them as one wielding a nameless authority. *(Chapter 11)*

Roger [...] carried death in his hands. *(Chapter 12)*

Activity 10

The rules, or lack of them, affect the boys differently during their time on the island. Complete the table below to show how the characters react differently to the lack of social boundaries.

Ralph	Jack	Piggy	Simon	Roger
			Always behaves in a positive way, reflecting his role as the moral centre of the novel.	

Tips for assessment

When you write about characters, remember that Golding has not presented them as one-dimensional. Ralph, for example, has a cruel side and Jack a sensitive side.

Minor characters

Samneric

Identical twins who **'seemed to share one wide, ecstatic grin'** *(Chapter 4)*, Samneric are the only boys other than Ralph and Piggy who do not choose to join Jack's tribe. When they do finally become members, it is because **"– they made us. They hurt us – "** *(Chapter 12)*. They are ashamed of the fact that they have defected to the tribe and try to help Ralph. However, they ultimately betray Ralph by revealing his hiding place to Jack. Samneric represent the idea that ordinary people can be forced to do things that they disagree with by more powerful figures.

The littluns

The littluns are mostly unnamed. To begin with, they are happy to follow Ralph because of his air of authority and his perceived connection to the adult world. They are easily frightened and firmly believe in the existence of the **"beastie"** *(Chapter 2)*. At first, they are willing to join in with Ralph's plans to build shelters but are soon **"off bathing, or eating, or playing"** *(Chapter 3)*. Eventually they are either seduced by the more easy-going way of life offered by Jack's tribe or frightened into joining.

The littluns eventually join Jack's tribe

> **Activity 11**
>
> Why do you think that Golding chose not to name all of the littluns? What do you think their purpose is in the novel?

The naval officer

The naval officer represents the adult world which Piggy thought would make things better. Dressed in **'a white-topped cap, and above the green shade of the peak was a crown, an anchor, gold foliage. [...] white drill, epaulettes, a revolver, a row of gilt buttons down the front of a uniform'** *(Chapter 12)*, the officer seems to be a kind of knight in shining armour come to the boys' rescue; he functions as a **deus ex machina**. However, he also represents the war which caused the boys to be on the island in the first place.

Told about the two deaths, he 'knew, as a rule, when people were telling the truth' *(Chapter 12)*, but still suggests that it has been a "Jolly good show. Like the Coral Island" *(Chapter 12)*. This suggests that he prefers to ignore the truth about the boys' actions. He represents those who persist in believing that evil is something that is only found elsewhere, rather than accepting that it is part of human nature.

> **deus ex machina** a plot device used to resolve a problem in the nick of time

The parachutist

At the end of Chapter 5, Ralph cries out for "something grown-up… a sign or something" as reassurance. The sign that he receives from the adult world at the start of Chapter 6 is a 'figure that hung with dangling limbs' – the dead parachutist. When Samneric find it, the dead parachutist assumes the form of the beast. It is only Simon who understands the significance of the body and frees it 'from the wind's indignity' *(Chapter 9)*.

The parachutist represents the idea that the adult world which the boys have invested such hope in is actually a hopeless place. The boys assume that any sign from the adult world will be positive and helpful, but the truth is that adults cannot be relied upon any more than the boys in the novel.

Activity 12

Look at the diagram below, which shows the changing relationships of the boys on the island. Complete the diagram, adding quotations from the text to demonstrate the boys' shifting loyalties.

Chapter 1	Chapter 2	Chapter 3
Piggy Ralph Simon Jack Littluns Choir	Piggy ←Allies→ Ralph Simon Jack Hunters	Piggy ←Allies→ Ralph Simon (More distance from Jack) More distance Jack Hunters

Writing about characters

Upgrade

In the novel, different characters symbolize different groups of people or individuals. Where relevant to the exam question, you should try to examine Golding's use of symbolism with reference to your own ideas.

Look at the answer below.

> Simon is an unusual character who the others find very difficult to understand. He likes to spend time alone and his epilepsy makes him different from the other boys. This makes him an outsider. William Golding calls him a 'Christ-figure'.

This tells the examiner that the student knows the text, but they haven't developed or supported their ideas nor have they explored Golding's intentions. Now look at this answer, which effectively analyses Golding's presentation of Simon.

> Simon is an outsider on the island. The others find him very difficult to understand because he likes to spend time 'utterly alone' (Chapter 3), and his epilepsy makes him different from the other boys. William Golding calls him a 'Christ-figure' and he displays Christian qualities of kindness and generosity throughout the novel. It is significant that he is the only character to understand that the beast is within them all and that he dies trying to tell them the truth.

Character map

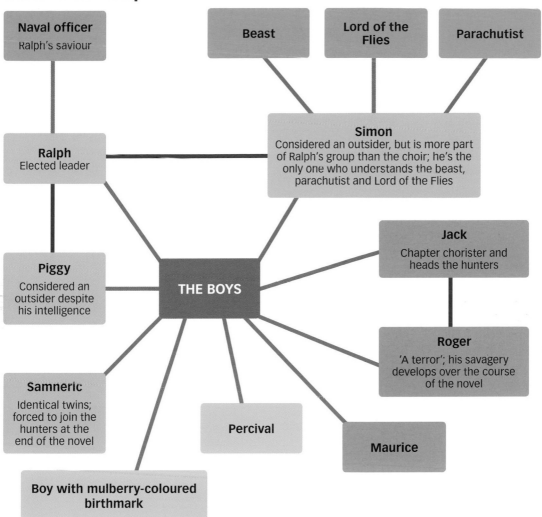

Naval officer
Ralph's saviour

Beast

Lord of the Flies

Parachutist

Simon
Considered an outsider, but is more part of Ralph's group than the choir; he's the only one who understands the beast, parachutist and Lord of the Flies

Ralph
Elected leader

THE BOYS

Jack
Chapter chorister and heads the hunters

Piggy
Considered an outsider despite his intelligence

Roger
'A terror'; his savagery develops over the course of the novel

Samneric
Identical twins; forced to join the hunters at the end of the novel

Percival

Maurice

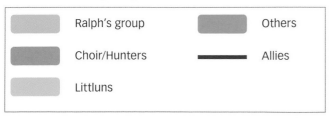

Boy with mulberry-coloured birthmark

Character map key

	Ralph's group		Others
	Choir/Hunters	———	Allies
	Littluns		

Perspectives

Lord of the Flies is narrated in the **third person** by an **omniscient narrator**. Golding's omniscient narration offers an overview of life on the island, allowing the reader to understand the thoughts and feelings of all of the characters, as well as witness events that occur in different places.

However, at times, Golding shifts the **perspective** to allow the reader to experience an event from more than one point of view. Golding often uses the linguistic technique of **free indirect speech** to provide the reader with greater insight into what each character is thinking. This device allows the reader to feel as though they are hearing the thoughts of the character directly.

> **free indirect speech** where a character's words or thoughts are conveyed directly, but without using speech marks or 'he/she said'
>
> **omniscient narrator** a narrator who knows everything about the characters, including their inner thoughts and motivations
>
> **perspective** point of view
>
> **third person** from the perspective of a character or voice outside the story, using the pronouns 'he' or 'she'

Key quotations

Again he fell into that strange mood of speculation that was so foreign to him. If faces were different when lit from above or below – what was a face? What was anything? *(Chapter 5)*

His mind skated to a consideration of a tamed town where savagery could not set foot. What could be safer than the bus centre with its lamps and wheels? *(Chapter 10)*

The officer inspected the little scarecrow in front of him. The kid needed a bath, a hair-cut, a nose-wipe and a good deal of ointment. *(Chapter 12)*

Interestingly, as the novel progresses, Golding increasingly relies on free indirect speech. As the boys struggle to communicate effectively with each other, Golding reveals more of their inner frustrations.

Activity 1

Find three examples of free indirect speech in the novel. For each example, consider:

a) why Golding has chosen to use the technique at this point

b) what we learn about the character's attitudes

c) what we learn about their relationships with other characters.

Tips for assessment

You need to be able to write about Golding's choice of language and the effects of those language choices. It is better to write that 'Golding's free indirect speech allows us to hear Ralph's thoughts directly and to empathize with him' than to write simply that 'Golding uses free indirect speech'.

In the last chapter, Golding switches from the viewpoint of the narrator to that of Ralph, allowing the reader to live through the fear of being chased with him. This shift also makes the event seem more immediate.

Activity 2

Omniscient narrator.

> Another double cry at the same distance gave him a clue to their plan. Any savage baulked in the forest would utter the double shout and hold up the line till he was free again. That way they might hope to keep the cordon unbroken right across the island. Ralph thought of the boar that had broken through them with such ease. If necessary, when the chase came too close, he could charge the cordon while it was still thin, burst through, and run back. But run back where? The cordon would turn and sweep again. Sooner or later he would have to sleep or eat – and then he would awaken with hands clawing at him; and the hunt would become a running down.

Golding reveals the extent of Ralph's fear through free indirect speech.

> What was to be done then? The tree? Burst the line like a boar? Either way the choice was terrible.

Point of view changes in this paragraph.

> A single cry quickened his heart-beat and, leaping up, he dashed away towards the ocean side and the thick jungle till he was hung up among creepers; he stayed there for a moment with his calves quivering. If only one could have pax, a long pause, a time to think!
>
> (Chapter 12)

1. Look closely at this extract. How does Golding use free indirect speech here and what is its effect?

2. What do you think the use of free indirect speech adds to the novel as a whole? Write a paragraph explaining your thoughts, including quotations to support your ideas.

3. Look at the extract again. How does Golding use language to control the pace and create tension? Consider the use of short sentences and questions.

Voices

Golding claimed that his intention in the novel was to 'make [the characters] real boys instead of paper cut-outs with no life in them'. To achieve this, he created a distinct **idiolect** for each of the boys.

Piggy

Golding gives Piggy the most distinctive voice in the novel. Ironically, although he is the most intelligent member of the group, Piggy's language is the most non-standard and is often littered with grammatical inaccuracies, for example: **"I got to have them specs. Now I only got one eye"** *(Chapter 4)*. Golding uses language to differentiate Piggy from the other boys and to mark him as an outsider from the beginning: **'Piggy was an outsider, not only by accent, which did not matter, but by fat, and ass-mar, and specs, and a certain disinclination for manual labour'** *(Chapter 4)*. It could be argued that his use of **colloquial** language and non-standard speech patterns reveals Piggy's lower social status.

Although Piggy is an outsider who often uses non-standard English, Ralph realizes that he has brains and envies his logical way of thinking

Jack

Jack speaks in a very assertive and aggressive manner. He uses **Standard English** (which may indicate his high social status and educational background) and often speaks in direct, decisive statements: **"We'll go into the forest now and hunt"** *(Chapter 8)*. The **imperative verb** is used frequently in his speech, which reflects his domineering and forceful nature: **"Do our dance! Come on! Dance!"** *(Chapter 9)*

colloquial informal, everyday speech

idiolect the individual speech patterns of a person

imperative verb command verbs, e.g. *'Do* our dance'

Standard English the form of English that is considered the norm and is typically used in formal situations

Activity 3

1. Find five typical examples of each of the following characters' speech:

   a) Ralph   **d)** Simon

   b) Jack   **e)** Roger.

   c) Piggy

   Consider carefully what their speech patterns suggest about each character.

2. How does Golding use the characters' voices to reveal the relationships and social hierarchies in the novel?

3. Many of the phrases that the characters use are now unfamiliar to us, but would have been in common use at the time. Look at the phrases below and, using their context to help you, work out what they mean.

   "All right choir. Take off your togs." *(Chapter 1)*

   " – if he gets waxy we've had it –" *(Chapter 11)*

   "This would make a wizard fort." *(Chapter 6)*

4. Find three more examples of **archaic** language used in the novel.

archaic old-fashioned

Naming

Over the course of the novel, Golding changes the way in which a number of the characters are named. For example, the twins are initially introduced as two separate people: **"Sam 'n Eric"** *(Chapter 1)*; however, as the novel progresses, they seem to become a single entity to the other boys and are simply referred to as **"Samneric"** *(Chapter 4)*. There is a sense that the twins start to lose their individual identities in the novel and Golding reflects this in the change of reference. Likewise, the small boys are first known as 'little 'uns' *(Chapter 2)*, but they soon become 'littluns' *(Chapter 3)* (with no 'e' or apostrophe). Although this is a subtle change, it suggests that as the social boundaries begin to break down on the island, so do the boundaries and rules which regulate language.

Activity 4

Names are an important aspect of the novel and Piggy's name, or lack of it, is significant.

Consider the name 'Piggy'.

a) What are the connotations of the name?

b) What do you think Golding wants the reader to understand about Piggy's character from the fact that we never hear his real name?

c) What do you think Golding wants the reader to understand about the other boys from the fact that they never hear or use his real name?

Creating atmosphere

Golding writes in a vivid way, which helps the reader to visualize the events on the island clearly. He uses a number of literary techniques to create a menacing atmosphere on the island from the outset.

Personification

One of the devices that Golding uses throughout the novel is **personification**. He describes the island and its natural surroundings as having human characteristics; it is consistently referred to as a live being, with its **'savage arm of heat'** *(Chapter 2)*. The natural landscape is depicted as a creature that appears actively to resist and threaten the boys.

> **personification** a type of metaphor where human qualities are given to objects or ideas

The boys imagine that the forest is 'full of claws' (*Chapter 6*) and contains a beast; it epitomizes the menace of the unknown

Activity 5

For each of the quotations below, explain how Golding uses language to create a menacing atmosphere on the island.

Key quotations

The great rock loitered, poised on one toe, decided not to return, moved through the air, fell, struck, turned over, leapt droning through the air... *(Chapter 1)*

Strange things happened at midday. The glittering sea rose up... *(Chapter 4)*

Soon the darkness was full of claws, full of the awful unknown and menace. *(Chapter 6)*

Activity 6

Look at the extract below. How does Golding create the impression that the fire has a life of its own? Make notes on the linguistic features that Golding uses and their effects, referring to the annotations to help you. You should look at Golding's use of:

- imagery and personification
- vocabulary
- sentence structure and length
- punctuation.

The fire seems to have a life of its own (personification).

Describes the fire as a squirrel (simile), which seems like an unusual comparison.

Suggests that the fire is destroying the tree as they watch.

Smoke was rising here and there among the creepers that festooned the dead or dying trees. As they watched, a flash of fire appeared at the root of one wisp, and then the smoke thickened. Small flames stirred at the bole of a tree and crawled away through leaves and brushwood, dividing and increasing. One patch touched a tree trunk and scrambled up like a bright squirrel. The smoke increased, sifted, rolled outwards. The squirrel leapt on the wings of the wind and clung to another standing tree, eating downwards. Beneath the dark canopy of leaves and smoke the fire laid hold on the forest and began to gnaw. Acres of black and yellow smoke rolled steadily towards the sea. At the sight of the flames and the irresistible course of the fire, the boys broke into shrill, excited cheering. The flames, as though they were a kind of wild life, crept as a jaguar creeps on its belly toward a line of birch-like saplings that fledged an outcrop of the pink rock. They flapped at the first of the trees, and the branches grew a brief foliage of fire. The heart of flame leapt nimbly across the gap between the trees and then went swinging and flaring along the whole row of them. Beneath the capering boys a quarter of a mile square of forest was savage with smoke and flame. The separate noises of the fire merged into a drum-roll that seemed to shake the mountain. *(Chapter 2)*

Activity 7

1. Look at the beginning of an answer below, which has been written in response to the question in Activity 6. Continue it, using your notes from Activity 6 to help you.

> When Golding describes the fire, he begins by using verbs such as 'stirred' and 'crawled' to suggest that it is like an animal. These verbs imply that it is small and easily controlled. To link with the idea that it is a small animal, he calls it a 'bright squirrel'. This makes the fire seem alive and exciting, and the word 'bright' seems positive. However...

2. Now find another example of Golding's use of extended personification in *Lord of the Flies*. Make notes on the linguistic features used and their effects, focusing specifically on how they add to the atmosphere in the text. Remember to look closely at Golding's use of:

   - imagery and personification
   - sentence structure and length
   - vocabulary
   - punctuation.

   When you have finished, write your notes up into a complete paragraph in the same manner as question 1.

Tips for assessment

To get high marks, you need to consider Golding's use of language in detail. It is important that you demonstrate that you have understood the literary techniques that Golding has employed and their effects.

Pathetic fallacy

Golding also uses pathetic fallacy to create atmosphere in the novel. In Chapter 9, the storm which builds and breaks during Simon's murder reflects the rising tension on the island. The unendurable noise of the storm and the **'blue-white scar'** *(Chapter 9)* of the lightning mirrors the frenzied state of the boys themselves. The aggressive force of the storm, which **'tore leaves and branches from the trees'** *(Chapter 9)*, echoes the violent actions of the boys.

The storm and lightning mirror the rising tension on the island and the increasingly frenzied state of the boys

Animalistic imagery

As the island becomes increasingly creature-like, the boys seem to become more and more animalistic. Golding uses a range of **similes** to highlight the animalistic behaviour of the boys, who are described as **'like dogs'** *(Chapter 2)* and **'ape-like among the tangle of trees'** *(Chapter 3)*. The animalistic **imagery** clearly hints at the boys' increasing savagery.

Golding takes his use of animalistic imagery one step further in his description of Simon's murder. The boys are no longer seen as human; they are simply reduced to **'teeth and claws'** *(Chapter 9)*. Golding has moved from using similes to describe the boys' similarity to animals to using **metaphorical** language; the implication is that the boys are no longer *like* animals, they have now *become* animals.

imagery descriptive language which builds up an image in the reader's mind, e.g. similes and metaphors

metaphor a comparison of one thing to another to make a description more vivid; a metaphor states that one thing *is* another

simile a comparison of one thing to another to make a description move vivid, using the words 'like' or 'as'

Activity 8

In Chapter 5, Piggy asks: **"What are we? Humans? Or animals? Or savages?"**

1. Find five examples of animalistic imagery in the novel. Note where each reference appears in the novel. For each one, consider why you think Golding has chosen that particular image.

2. How does Golding's use of animal imagery develop and change as the novel progresses? Why do you think this is? (Hint: look closely at the use of similes and metaphors.)

Juxtaposition

Golding uses **juxtaposition** to represent the conflict between civilization and savagery in *Lord of the Flies* and also to show the tension between opposing feelings and impulses. For example, Ralph and Jack are described as having conflicting feelings for one another; they are **'baffled, in love and hate'** *(Chapter 3)*. This conflict between love and hate adds to the sense of tension on the island.

juxtaposition two opposite ideas placed side by side to emphasize the link or the difference between them

Golding juxtaposes the characters of Ralph and Jack in the novel.

Key quotations

Unwillingly Ralph turned away from the splendid, awful sight.
(Chapter 2)

Activity 9

Find three more examples of juxtaposition in the novel. For each example, consider:

a) why Golding has chosen to use the technique at this point

b) what it reveals about the character's relationships and conflicts in the novel.

Writing about language

Upgrade

When you write about the text, you will need to be able to explain how Golding has used language and to what effect.

Even if language is not formally assessed in your question, you will need to show that you understand how Golding has used language to develop his characters, ideas and themes.

Questions which have 'how' in them mean that you need to consider the techniques that Golding has used in the novel. Many of the techniques will relate to Golding's use of language.

To get high marks, you will need to be able to pick out specific words and phrases, and explore them in detail in relation to the question.

Civilization and savagery

In *Lord of the Flies*, Golding considers the complex relationship between civilization and savagery. By the end of the novel, he seems to have concluded that savagery is inherent; Simon's 'conversation' with the Lord of the Flies in Chapter 8 reveals that evil is **"part of you"** rather than being something external. Ralph appears to have grasped this concept by the novel's conclusion when he admits to Piggy: **"I'm frightened. Of us"** *(Chapter 10)*.

The change from civilized boys to savages is very subtle in the novel. To begin with, the boys operate in a civilized way: they have been conditioned by their backgrounds to behave in an organized and efficient manner. The boys initially try to copy the behaviour of adults by establishing rules and voting for a leader. They recognize the importance of behaving in an adult way so that they can be rescued.

Key quotations

"Aren't there any grown-ups?"

"No."

Merridew sat down on a trunk and looked round the circle.

"Then we'll have to look after ourselves." *(Chapter 1)*

Over time, the savage behaviour of the boys gradually worsens as they abandon the social codes by which they previously lived and the rules that they have established on the island. As some of the boys start to realize that the **'taboo of the old life'** *(Chapter 4)* and the **'protection of parents and school and policemen and the law'** *(Chapter 4)* no longer apply, they begin to forget their old life; Jack, for example, **'had to think for a moment before he could remember what rescue was'** *(Chapter 3)*.

On a simple level, the conflict between Ralph and Jack can be seen as representative of the wider conflict between civilization and savagery in the novel. The conch, which Ralph uses to assemble the

The conch is a symbol of fairness and democracy in the novel

boys, becomes a symbol of fairness and democracy, and is seen as a powerful link to the civilized world. Once the conch is destroyed, the boys' descent into savagery accelerates. The mask, on the other hand, which is adopted by Jack, frees their animalistic urges and transforms them into **'painted savages'** *(Chapter 11).*

Activity 1

The conch is symbolic of democracy and civilized behaviour in the novel, whereas the mask is representative of savagery. Complete the table below to show how references to the mask and conch help to develop the theme of civilization and savagery throughout the novel.

	Chapter 1	Chapter 2	Chapter 3
Civilization	Boys wear clothes. Even though they take some of them off, they dress again.		
References to the conch	Ralph finds and uses the conch to call the others. It is used as a means of controlling the meetings and making them democratic.		
Savagery		Jack likes the idea of rules because he wants to hand out punishments.	
References to the mask			

Activity 2

1. Golding wants us to understand that becoming savage is not something that happens overnight, but is rather something that may happen gradually over time. Find five examples of the increasingly savage and barbaric actions of the boys in *Lord of the Flies*.

2. Write an answer to the following question, using the examples that you found for question 1 as evidence: How does Golding show that everyone has the capacity for evil and how does he develop this over the course of the novel?

Clothing

The boys' clothes become a clear indicator of the extent to which they have abandoned their past civilized lives. The boys begin to lose their **inhibitions** as their appearance deteriorates.

At the beginning of the novel, the characters' clothing represents their link with **'a civilization […] in ruins'** *(Chapter 4)*; despite the searing heat, the choir arrive in black cloaks and Ralph insists on re-dressing after his swim in Chapter 1. As the novel progresses, the boys begin to abandon their clothes, while Jack's adoption of the mask marks a turning point in his descent into bloodthirsty savagery. Ralph, naively, still believes in the civilizing power of clothing at the end of the novel when he approaches Jack's tribe. In Chapter 11 he hopes that approaching the tribe **'looking like we used to, washed and hair brushed'** will prove that **'we aren't savages really and being rescued isn't a game'**.

Like the boys' clothes, Piggy's glasses are explicitly linked to the civilization that they have left behind: the glasses are their only means of lighting the fire and therefore of being rescued. However, noticeably, as the condition of the glasses deteriorates, so too does the behaviour of the boys on the island.

When the hunters abandon their clothes and paint their faces and bodies their behaviour deteriorates into savagery

inhibitions the subconscious rules by which the boys previously lived

---

Key quotations

The fair boy stopped and jerked his stockings with an automatic gesture that made the jungle seem for a moment like the Home Counties. *(Chapter 1)*

... the mask was a thing on its own, behind which Jack hid, liberated from shame and self-consciousness. *(Chapter 4)*

[Ralph] noticed – in this new mood of comprehension – how the folds were stiff like cardboard, and unpleasant; noticed too how the frayed edges of his shorts were making an uncomfortable, pink area on the front of his thighs. With a convulsion of the mind, Ralph discovered dirt and decay... *(Chapter 5)*

Activity 3

At the novel's conclusion, Golding juxtaposes the pristine appearance of the officer with the unkempt appearance of Ralph and the other boys. This serves to highlight the extent to which the boys have changed. Complete the table below to show how the boys' appearance and the level of savagery on the island develop over the course of the novel.

	Chapter 1	Chapter 2		Chapter 12
Savagery				'their bodies streaked with coloured clay'
Civilization	'To put on a grey shirt once more was strangely pleasing.'			'white drill, epaulettes, a revolver, a row of gilt buttons down the front of a uniform'

Symbolism

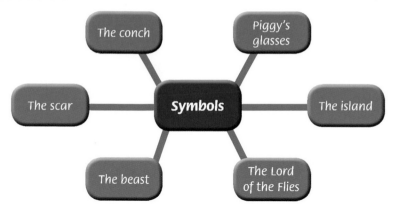

Lord of the Flies is an **allegorical** novel. Golding's presentation of characters, events and objects is deeply symbolic. His use of symbolism in the novel helps to develop the theme of civilization and savagery. In his essay, 'Fable', Golding commented that he wanted to show that 'one lot of people is inherently like any other lot of people; and the only enemy of man is inside him'.

allegory a story with a hidden meaning in which characters, events and objects have a symbolic function

Activity 4

Dictatorship

Extreme behaviour

Intelligence

Civilization

Man's negative impact on the world

The devil

Knowledge

The world

The evil within everyone

Vision

Reason

1. The ideas above are represented in the novel through various symbols (see spider diagram). Try to match the symbols from the spider diagram above with these ideas, finding a suitable quotation to support your answer. There will be five ideas left over.

2. Each of the five remaining ideas is represented by a character in the novel. Try to work out which character is representative of each of the five ideas.

3. The symbols in the novel develop as the novel progresses. Complete the table opposite to show how and why Golding presents these changes.

Symbol	Chapter 1	Chapter 2	Chapter 3
The conch		'Piggy, partly recovered, pointed to the conch in Ralph's hands, and Jack and Simon fell silent. Ralph went on.'	
Piggy's glasses			
The island			"As if it wasn't a good island."
The scar	'Beyond falls and cliffs there was a gash visible in the trees'		
The beast			
The Lord of the Flies			

Tips for assessment

Upgrade

When you write about a theme, make sure that you write about how the theme develops in the novel. You should consider why Golding has presented the theme as he has.

Games

To begin with life on the island is very much like a game to the boys. The election is described as a toy and the littluns spend much of their day building sandcastles. However, the innocent games of the boys soon turn into something more sinister and, by the end of the novel, the increasing brutality of the boys' games mirrors their increasing barbarity and savagery. The re-enactment of the pig hunt in Chapter 7 begins as a game but quickly escalates: **'Robert squealed in mock terror, then in real pain.'** This idea is echoed elsewhere in the novel; for example, the killing of Simon follows a frenzied celebration of the tribe's hunt. It is clear that the boundary between playing and killing becomes increasingly blurred; at the end of the novel, the officer asks whether they were **"Having a war or something"** *(Chapter 12)*, further emphasizing this link between murder and play.

Having worked themselves into a frenzy and mistaking him for the beast, the boys kill Simon (as seen here in a 2011 theatre production)

Key quotations

Might it not be possible to walk boldly into the fort, say – "I've got pax," laugh lightly and sleep among the others? Pretend they were still boys, schoolboys who had said "Sir, yes, Sir" – and worn caps? *(Chapter 12)*

Activity 5

1. Make a list of all of the games that the boys play in the novel.

2. Identify whether each game transforms into something more threatening. Here is an example to get you started:

> Littluns building sandcastles is just a game – but Roger and Maurice deliberately destroy them – 'kicking them over'. They 'made no protest' so Roger sees that he can get away with doing cruel things.

Power and leadership

Gaining and maintaining power is central to the novel. Initially, the idea of having a chief is to have someone to decide things. At this stage, power is given democratically: the boys vote for Ralph, although they consider voting a **'toy'** *(Chapter 1)*. It is clear that they do not take power or the means of granting power very seriously in the beginning; it is simply a game to them. Although they elect Ralph, it is the conch that they are **'most obscurely, yet most powerfully'** drawn to *(Chapter 1)*.

From the outset, Jack makes it clear that possessing power is important to him. He assumes that because he has been a leader at school, this automatically makes him leader on the island: **'"I ought to be chief," said Jack, with simple arrogance'** *(Chapter 1)*. He fails to realize that the skills which make him a good chorister are not the skills needed for a leader on the island. He also does not recognize that he is not particularly popular on the island, even among the choir.

Activity 6

1. The power relationships between the boys shift over the course of the novel. The diagram below shows the hierarchy at the start. Draw a new diagram to represent the power structure at the end of the novel.

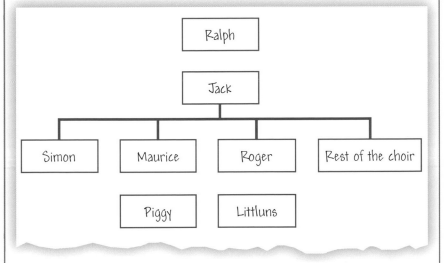

2. Consider the importance of rules in the novel. Does Golding suggest that rules are necessary for a successful society? Use quotations from the novel to support your ideas.

Tips for assessment

You will see that the themes in the novel don't stand alone: there are many links between them. Make sure that you consider this in your answers.

While Ralph feels the burden of responsibility and worries that he is not a good leader, **'He was vexed to find how little he thought like a grown-up'** *(Chapter 8)*, Jack becomes obsessed with assuming leadership. He resents Ralph's position and the respect that the other boys have for him. When Ralph stands his ground over the rebuilding of the fire in Chapter 4, **'Jack was powerless and raged without knowing why'**. A power struggle ensues as Jack challenges Ralph's authority directly in Chapter 5: **"Who are you, anyway? Sitting there – telling people what to do. You can't hunt, you can't sing –"**.

Jack manipulates situations to enhance his own power, making the most of opportunities to undermine Ralph and to turn the other boys against him. For example, he uses dishonest tactics by claiming that Ralph **"thinks you're cowards, running away from the boar and the beast"** *(Chapter 8)*. When Jack does finally assume power of the rival tribe, he controls the boys in a dictatorial fashion. Likewise, he manipulates the boys' fear of the beast to ensure that they cooperate with him. Even though he recognizes that the beast does not exist and that they actually killed Simon, he insists that **"[The beast] may come again […] So watch"** *(Chapter 10)*. His tribe are described as **'Half-relieved, half-daunted by the implication of further terrors'** *(Chapter 10)*.

Activity 7

The famous historian Lord Acton once said that 'power tends to corrupt, and absolute power corrupts absolutely'. Consider the characters who possess power in the novel. Do you think that Lord Acton's statement applies to them? Give evidence from the text to support your ideas.

Fear

Fear is used as a weapon on the island to assume and maintain power. Ralph uses the fear of not being rescued to persuade the boys to tend to the fire. In this case, he is using fear to influence the boys to do the right thing – it is for their own benefit: **"How can we ever be rescued except by luck, if we don't keep a fire going?"** *(Chapter 5)*. Jack, on the other hand, uses the fear of the beast and later the fear of punishment to make people join his tribe. This shows the difference in their characters and leadership styles.

It is Roger who ultimately inspires the most fear in the novel. Although Golding directly tells the reader very little, he makes it clear that Roger has the ability to be exceptionally cruel; he is described as **"a terror"** *(Chapter 12)*. We are left in little

Simon's conversation with the Lord of the Flies confirms that the boys are most afraid of the evil within themselves

doubt that he would have eventually taken the chieftainship for himself since, by the end of the novel, he is taking a leading role within the tribe and **'only just avoid[s] pushing [Jack] with his shoulder'** *(Chapter 11)*. The power that Roger possesses is arguably even more dangerous than Jack's because he seems not to have any boundaries.

Fear is ever-present on the island. The littluns' **irrational** fear, in Chapter 2, of the **"beastie"** that **"came in the dark"** increases throughout the novel. Although it is clear to the reader that there is no beast, it remains an important idea within the novel. As well as being a tool that Jack uses to manipulate others, the beast is also a reflection of the boys' own capacity for evil. The discovery of the parachutist and the exaggeration which follows only serve to strengthen this idea. Simon is the only one who understands what they are really afraid of: themselves and each other. When he hears the voice of the Lord of the Flies, it confirms what he already knew.

> **Key quotations**
>
> **"Fancy thinking the Beast was something you could hunt and kill!"** said the head. [...] **"You knew, didn't you? I'm part of you? Close, close, close! I'm the reason why it's no go? Why things are what they are?"**
> *(Chapter 8)*

irrational without reason or logic

Activity 8

1. The fear that is present on the island escalates and diminishes at different points in the novel. Complete the chart below to show how fear increases and decreases over the course of the novel.

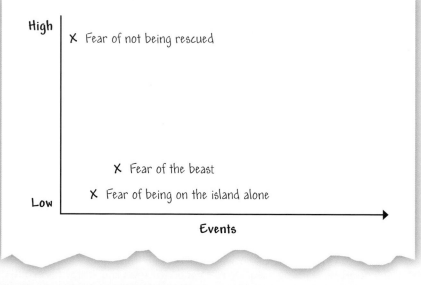

2. When you have completed your chart:

   a) Add quotations to support each of the points that you have added.

   b) Colour code the points to indicate which character is feeling the fear.

   c) Colour code the points to indicate which character is responsible for the fear.

Connecting themes

The themes in the novel are interconnected. Some of them fit together especially well; for example, savagery and power.

Activity 9

Using the themes discussed, develop a table which shows how the different themes link together. You could use a table like this.

	Civilization	Savagery	Fear	Power and leadership	Games
Civilization					
Savagery					
Fear				Fear is a means of control – Ralph uses fear of being stranded on the island to make the boys care about the fire.	
Power and leadership					
Games		The killing of Simon begins as a game but gets out of hand.			

Writing about themes

Upgrade

You need to be able to trace themes throughout the novel and explain how Golding uses different characters and events to develop these themes.

Even if the question is not specifically about themes in the novel, you should still show that you have understood them. For example, if you are writing about the character of Jack, you can show how Golding tackles the themes of civilization, savagery and power through the way he behaves and what he says.

You should look at how a theme develops as the novel progresses. For example, is the theme of power more important at the end of the novel than at the beginning? What does this suggest about the novel as a whole? You might also consider whether certain events in the story make a particular theme more prominent and how different characters relate to the theme at different times.

Skills and Practice

Exam skills

Understanding the question

Before you begin your assessment, you should look at the number of marks awarded to each section of the question. Then divide the time you have available for the answer in proportion to the marks. For example, if you have 45 minutes to answer a two-part question where part a) is worth 7 marks and part b) is worth 20 marks, it is clear that you should spend no more than ten minutes on part a) and about 30 minutes on part b) – allowing five minutes for planning. If the two parts are worth 10 marks each, you should aim to spend 20 minutes on each part.

Try to approach the question methodically. Start by identifying what the question is actually asking you to do: you could underline the key words and phrases, and note down what they mean. Examiners use certain words and phrases quite often. Learn what they mean and they will tell you what you need to write about:

'**Explore**' means look at all the different aspects of something. For example, 'Explore how the author presents Piggy' means you need to look at Piggy's character when he is with different people; how and why he might be different in those situations; and the way in which the author describes him when he is presented on his own.

'**How does the author...**' or '**show how...**' means explain the techniques the author uses to create an effect. For example, 'How does Golding present fear in this extract?' means you need to look at how he builds up suspense or tension in the way in which the extract is structured. Think about the language used and pick out details such as verbs and passages of description. Also look at how different characters react to the situation and how that helps the reader to feel the fear.

'**Present**' and '**portray**' are similar words for looking at a character and prompt you to consider not only what the character is like, but also what devices the author uses to show this. For example, 'How is Jack presented/portrayed?' means you need to say how he is described; what Golding makes him say and do, and why; how other people react to him; and how he shows Jack as important to the story.

'**In what ways...**' means look at different sides of something. For example, 'In what ways is Simon significant?' means you need to look at more than just the fact that he is killed by the boys. You need to explain what his attitude to the beast is and how and why different characters respond to him in different ways, for example.

'**How far**' means the examiner wants you to evaluate the extent of something. For example, 'How far do you agree that the conflict between Jack and Ralph is at the heart of the novel?' means that you need to analyse the conflict between Jack and Ralph; how their conflict is a representation of the struggle between civilization and savagery; and how these ideas are linked to an exploration of the beast. You need to make sure that you consider a range of ideas but come back to the original question and say whether you agree or disagree that it is central.

'What role...' means write not just about the character and how they are shown, but also about their function in the novel. For example, 'What role does Roger play?' means you have to write about his character and how it is shown, but also why he is in the novel at all (try imagining the novel without him). To begin with, he seems not to be very important, but this changes as the novel develops. He demonstrates casual cruelty to the littluns. He shows the impact that lack of consequences can have and what might happen if people are left to their own devices for too long. He is the most evil of the characters on the island and we sense that there would be more to come from him if the officer had not arrived.

'Explain' or **'comment on'** invites you to give your response to something in as much detail as you can. For example, 'Explain the importance of the idea of civilization in the novel' means you should write about how the boys feel about keeping hold of their civilized behaviour; the methods they use to try to do so; and what prevents them from doing this. You should also write about what happens when civilization starts to break down.

Look at the question below. The key words have been highlighted and explained.

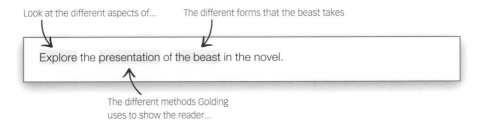

Look at the different aspects of...   The different forms that the beast takes

Explore the presentation of the beast in the novel.

The different methods Golding uses to show the reader...

You are being asked to do a number of things in this question. You need to look at the methods Golding uses to:

- introduce the beast
- show the littluns' reactions
- show the older boys' reactions
- demonstrate the different forms that the beast takes for different characters
- reveal the symbolic significance of the beast.

Activity 1

1. Consider the question below.

   Show how Piggy is important to the novel as a whole.

   a) Highlight or underline the key words and phrases, and then describe what you are being asked to do.

   b) Make a bullet list of things you need to do to answer the question.

Planning your answer

It is worth taking five minutes to plan your answer before you start to write it. This section looks at two different ways of planning an essay: lists and spider diagrams. Either of these plans would help you to gather ideas for your answer and help structure your response.

Tips for assessment

Don't spend your revision time preparing possible answers to almost every question in advance. Examiners always make the point that candidates who use their own ideas about the text produce fresher and more interesting answers.

Lists

You can list points that you want to include, perhaps with a brief note of the evidence you will use. Remember you need to ensure that each point focuses on the question. You could do this by arranging your list in two columns. This is what a two-column list might look like for the following question:

> **Explore the presentation of Simon in the novel.**

Technique (presentation)	Effects (what it tells us about Simon)
1. Initially presented in a negative way by Jack: "He's always throwing a faint"	1. Suggests Simon is an outsider from the beginning
2. Negative connotations of other boys' descriptions of Simon: "queer. He's funny."	2. People don't understand him and yet they generally treat him better than they treat Piggy, for example
3. Simon's understanding of the human nature of the beast: "maybe it's only us"	3. He has a greater understanding of human nature than the other boys
4. The manner in which Simon foretells events, e.g. his own death, Ralph's rescue	4. Simon displays an almost mystical insight, which is linked to his position as a 'Christ-like' figure
5. Simon's conversation with the Lord of the Flies	5. Develops the idea that Simon possesses insight and also draws on the religious parallels between the character and Christ
6. Simon's treatment of the parachutist: 'poor broken thing'	6. This shows his empathy and kindness
7. Symbolism of his death	7. Shows the depths of the boys' depravity; symbolic of the end of civilization

Activity 2

Create a two-column plan for each of the following questions.

a) To what extent do you think Ralph is to blame for what goes wrong on the island?

b) What role does the adult world play in the novel as a whole?

c) Explain the importance of the conch in the novel.

Spider diagrams

You could also put your points into a spider diagram. Again, you need to ensure that your plan remains focused on the key words of the question: 'Explore' (i.e. look at the different aspects), 'presentation' (i.e. the techniques Golding uses) and 'Simon'.

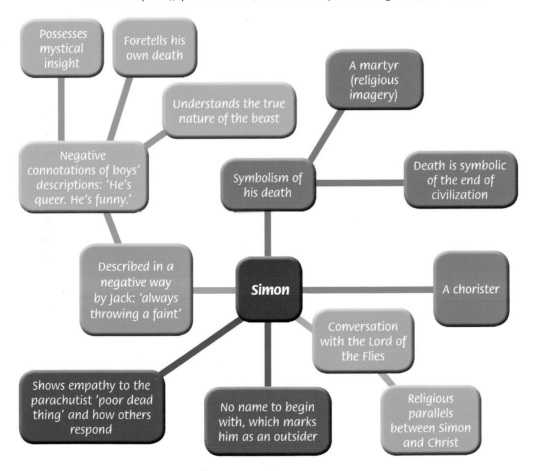

Activity 3

Use a spider diagram to plan an answer to each of the following questions.

a) What is the significance of violence in *Lord of the Flies*?

b) How is Jack presented in *Lord of the Flies*?

Tips for assessment

Plan your time carefully in the exam. Don't spend too long on your plan or you will run out of time to complete your answer.

Don't cross out your plan, because if you do run out of time you may be given credit for it.

Writing your answer

Once you have a good plan, you will have a clear idea of what you need to write to answer the question effectively. It might be helpful to prioritize your points by highlighting which ones you would like to cover first. You should also have an idea in mind for how you intend to finish your answer.

When you write, it is important that you make correct use of spelling, punctuation and grammar.

Using PEE (Point, Evidence, Explanation)

Examiners want to see that you can support your ideas in a thoughtful way and that you have based them on what the writer says and means. For example, in your answer you might make the point:

> Simon wants people to understand that the beast is not a creature with claws.

Your evidence for this might be:

> He shows this when he tries to explain that "maybe it's only us".

Your explanation might be:

> The language he uses is simple, which suggests that this is an obvious idea to Simon and one which should be obvious to the other boys too. This shows that he is brave, because he knows that this will not be a popular idea, but he feels that he should do the right thing.

Tips for assessment

Upgrade

While PEE is a helpful reminder of what you need to build into your writing, you do not need to follow this pattern for every single point you make. It is useful for the important points, but you should avoid getting bogged down with unnecessary repetition. To reach the higher grades, you need to control your argument and try to keep your answer flowing.

Using quotations

This is an important part of using evidence in your answer. Examiners want to see that you can select appropriate quotations that back up the point you are making. When you make a point, ask yourself: 'How do I know this?' Usually it will be because of something the author has written – this is the quotation you need.

For example, you might make the point:

> Simon sees the world differently from the other boys.

How do you know this? Well, there might be a number of quotations you could choose, but here is one:

> In Chapter 3, Golding describes how he likes to go off on his own: 'He looked over his shoulder [...] and glanced swiftly round to confirm that he was utterly alone.'

By choosing this quotation you will show that you:

- can select a relevant quotation to support your answer
- have understood how the fact that he likes being on his own makes him different
- have understood that this relates to an important theme of the book.

To show skills of a higher level, try to use embedded quotations. These short quotations (usually only a few words long) are easy to build into the flow of your own writing and you can also analyse them closely. For example:

> While the other boys don't want to challenge Ralph or Jack, Simon thinks it a 'perilous necessity' that he tell the truth even if it makes the other boys look unfavourably on him.

Embedded quotations appear within the main text of your writing and they are marked using quotation marks in the same way.

What not to do in an exam answer

✗ Do not begin with introductions such as 'In this essay I am going to...'. Get on with answering the question straightaway.

✗ Do not write a long introduction showing what you know about the author. Make just a brief reference and only if it is relevant to a point you are making.

✗ Do not write lengthy paragraphs about the background to the novel. You may think that information about empire and social class are important in the novel, but you only need to show this briefly while you focus on answering the question.

✗ Do not go into the exam with a prepared list of points and write about them regardless of whether they are relevant to the question.

✗ Do not run out of time to finish your answer – a plan will help you avoid this. It is better to focus on a detailed answer on a small part of the text than to try and make lots of different points.

✗ Do not try to write everything you know about the text. Make sure that you only choose things that are relevant to the question.

Achieving the best marks

Upgrade

To achieve high marks, you will need to do the following:

- show an assured or perceptive understanding of the book's themes/ideas
- show a pertinent or convincing response to the text
- select evidence that is relevant, detailed and sustained
- make references to context that are pertinent, convincing and supported by sustained relevant textual reference
- use sentences that are sophisticated and varied; show precise control of expression and meaning; use a full range of punctuation and spelling that is consistently accurate.

In practice this means that you need to show that you have understood the book on more than one level. On the surface, it is a story about some boys who have been stranded on an island and what happens to them while they are there. If you look more deeply, it is about human nature.

In addition, you will have to show an awareness and understanding of the author's techniques. You need to show that you understand the narrative structure, such as why Golding chose to have the story told by a narrator who is not part of the action. You will also need to show that you have considered the significant features of the text, such as the use of dialogue and how Golding uses this to present characters and reveal relationships. For every technique you identify, you need to show how and why Golding uses it and the effect it has on the reader.

Sample questions

1

Foundation Tier

Lord of the Flies

Answer part a) and **either** part b) **or** part c).

a) Look at the extract from Chapter 2 which begins "You got your small fire all right" and ends 'Jack dragged his eyes away from the fire.'

What thoughts and feelings do you have as you read this extract? Give reasons for what you say and remember to support your answer with words and phrases from the extract.

Either

b) What do you think about Piggy?
Think about:
- the way he speaks and behaves at different points in the novel
- how other characters treat him
- the way he is described.

Or

c) "We've got to have rules and obey them. After all, we're not savages." Write about some of the incidents from the novel which either support or do not support this statement. Give reasons for what you say.

2

Higher Tier

Lord of the Flies

Answer part a) and **either** part b) **or** part c).

a) Look at the extract from Chapter 2 which begins "You got your small fire all right" and ends 'Jack dragged his eyes away from the fire.'

With close reference to the extract, show how William Golding creates mood and atmosphere here.

Either

b) What do you think of Piggy and the way he is presented in the novel?

Or

c) "We've got to have rules and obey them. After all, we're not savages." To what extent do you agree that following the rules is an important idea in the novel? Remember to support your answer with detailed reference to the text.

7

Foundation Tier

Lord of the Flies

Look at the extract from Chapter 4 which begins 'Jack was standing under a tree about ten yards away' and ends with 'The mask compelled them.'

Answer **either** a) **or** b).

a) With reference to the extract and elsewhere in the novel, write about how Jack is presented.

In your answer, you should consider the presentation of:
- his actions and behaviour in the extract
- his actions and behaviour elsewhere in the novel
- the ways in which other characters respond to him.

b) Show how the idea of the beast becomes more important as the novel progresses.

In your answer, you should consider:
- when the beast is first mentioned
- how the beast is presented differently at different times in the novel
- how the boys respond to the beast
- what the beast represents.

8

Higher Tier

Lord of the Flies

Look at the extract from Chapter 4 which begins 'Jack was standing under a tree about ten yards away' and ends with 'The mask compelled them.'

Answer **either** a) **or** b).

a) With reference to the extract and elsewhere in the novel, write about the ways in which Jack is presented in the novel.

b) With reference to the ways Golding presents characters and events in the novel, show how the idea of the beast becomes more important as the novel progresses.

Sample answers

Sample answer 1

Below you will find a sample answer from a **Foundation Tier** student, together with examiner comments, to the following question on the novel:

> Discuss the idea that the conflict between Ralph and Jack is central to the novel.
>
> Write about:
> - what causes the conflict
> - what happens to show that there is conflict
> - how other characters react to the conflict
> - how Golding presents the conflict.

Accurate point but it needs a quotation.

Needs supporting with evidence.

Accurate point but it needs a quotation.

Recognizes the fact that Ralph replaces an adult in the eyes of the younger boys.

The conflict between Ralph and Jack is very important to the novel. The conflict is caused because they both want to be leader. Ralph looks a bit bigger than Jack and Ralph blows the conch to call the first meeting. The boys are impressed by Ralph because he takes charge and tells them what to do. They are scared and need someone to look up to. Ralph is older than most of the others and the little ones listen to him like he is a big brother or teacher. Ralph has the conch and one of the boys says "Let him be chief with the trumpet-thing" and so Ralph becomes chief.

Good choice of quotation in support but could be developed further.

Good point – it's important to recognize the effect on the reader.

A good point which could easily have been developed more fully.

There seems like there will be trouble from the start when Ralph tells Jack that "The choir belongs" to him. This makes the reader feel that Ralph knows how much Jack wanted to be chief and that he is trying to make sure that there is no conflict. When they explore the island for the first time, Ralph and Jack seem like a team and at the first proper meeting they seem to agree about the rules. However, Jack wants the rules so that people can be punished and Ralph wants them so that they can survive until they get rescued, which shows that there is a conflict in their ideas about how things should be done.

This could be traced further. It is a recurring theme.

In Chapter 3, the conflict is about building the huts. Jack and the choir have become hunters and have left Ralph and the others to build huts for them all. When Ralph asks Jack to help, Jack tells him "We want meat" and Ralph replies "And we don't get it." This is a criticism of Jack's hunting and Jack doesn't take criticism very well. 'The antagonism was audible' shows that there is conflict between them over this issue.

When the hunters let the fire go out in Chapter 4, it is because they are too busy hunting. This means that the ship that Ralph sees in the distance doesn't see them and this makes him angry. When he confronts Jack about it, Jack eventually apologizes. The hunters 'were of the opinion that Jack had done the right thing, had put himself in the right by his generous apology and Ralph, obscurely, in the wrong'. This makes Jack feel like he is more powerful than Ralph, so Ralph has to show that he is boss. To do this, he refuses to move so they have to build the fire somewhere else. This makes Jack angry: 'Ralph asserted his chieftainship and could not have chosen a better way if he had thought for days. Against this weapon, so indefinable and so effective, Jack was powerless and raged without knowing why.'

A long quotation which could have been looked at more closely.

One of the other conflicts between them is over Piggy. Ralph likes him and Jack doesn't. Whenever Ralph sticks up for Piggy about something, Jack feels that he is being overlooked, and whenever Piggy sticks up for Ralph, he feels that he is being criticized. When the fire goes out and has to be lit again, Ralph uses Piggy's glasses and 'Not even Ralph knew how a link between him and Jack had been snapped and fastened elsewhere.' This shows that the conflict between him and Jack will get worse because the link between them has been broken and Ralph is now more connected to Piggy.

Evidence would be helpful here.

The biggest conflict is when Jack challenges the rules. He is tired of being bossed around by Ralph and wants to hunt all the time. He says "Bollocks to the rules!" and leaves with lots of the other boys. This divides the group into people who want to follow rules and people who don't. Later on, in Chapter 8, when Jack wants to be elected chief over Ralph and the boys don't support him, he storms off. This makes the conflict worse because he knows that everyone thinks Ralph is a better leader and he doesn't like it when he's not in charge.

Too colloquial for an essay.

It would have been worthwhile to look closely at why this word was chosen and what effect it would have had.

The conflict between Ralph and Jack is very important in the novel because this conflict leads to the violence that takes place. The boys are very different types of leader and Golding wants to tell us that without rules people can become like savages.

A clearly written conclusion.

This answer shows that the candidate knows the text well and can trace a theme through it. They have used quotations to support their ideas but more references to the text are needed. Some of Golding's language use is commented on, but more thought needs to be given to the choice of words made by the author to present the conflict.

Sample answer 2

Below you will find a sample answer from a **Higher Tier** student, together with examiner comments, to the following question on the novel:

> To what extent do you agree that violence is at the heart of *Lord of the Flies*?

Sets the scene and presents the opposing view to that in the question.

Refers to language technique.

Links to the context.

To begin with, 'the jungle seem[s] [...] like the Home Counties'. The boys are used to existing within a rigidly structured society in which right and wrong, good and evil are obvious and controlled by adults. Initially, the boys work together and are supportive of one another but as they are alone and isolated, it is not long before things begin to go wrong. Despite Jack's assertion that "we're not savages. We're English; and the English are best at everything. So we've got to do the right things" they divide themselves into gangs or tribes and then the violence begins. They use pejorative language to talk about savages, which may suggest that they have been brought up to believe that foreign people are brutal and dangerous. The early juxtaposition of the British and savages as binary opposites suggests that the boys do not understand the truth about human nature and behaviour; in fact, their behaviour in the novel proves that their belief that the British are best and would not behave as savages is wrong.

Uses an embedded quotation well.

Clearly analyses Golding's language.

Embedded quotations are well chosen.

Early on in the novel, Jack and his group of hunters decide to catch and kill a pig in order to provide the group with meat. At this early stage, Jack is unable to commit the deed 'because of the unbearable blood', but we are told that 'Next time there would be no mercy.' Eventually, they do manage to track down a sow and throw wooden spears at her, causing her some injury. Following her, they surround and brutally kill her. This is not the humane slaughter of a creature for food, but a killing crazed by blood-lust. Golding describes how the scene was 'full of sweat and noise and blood and terror. [...] Roger found a lodgment for his point and began to push till he was leaning with his whole weight. The spear moved forward inch by inch and the terrified squealing became a high-pitched scream.' The use of the adjective 'terrified' shows the barbarity of the act and the vivid description of Roger 'leaning with his whole weight' implies that he is calmly and deliberately terrorizing the animal. In no way is this simply a kill for food. The boys are enjoying the kill and are 'heavy and fulfilled' when it is over. The violence of this event is extreme. This shows the reader that the boys have moved far from their initial ideas of civilization and are now entering the realms of savagery, which they claimed to reject earlier in the novel. While they do need to kill for food, they do not need to do so in such a violent and brutal manner.

Uses appropriate terminology well.

This incident foreshadows worse events to come. Jack orders that a stick be sharpened at both ends so that the pig's decapitated head can be impaled upon it as a gift for the beast. Samneric tell Ralph in Chapter 12 that 'Roger sharpened a stick at both ends'. This hints at the violence he plans to use against Ralph; there are clear connotations of deliberate and cold-blooded torture.

Link to another appropriate event in text shows that the candidate knows the novel well.

Violence is also brought about by hysteria. In Chapter 9, Jack uses his tribal dance to try to control the boys when it looks as if his hunters might leave him to return to Ralph. He orders them to "Do our dance!" The fact that he uses the imperative makes it hard for them to resist and means that they are almost forced to join in. Golding uses pathetic fallacy to build the tension in this scene: as the storm is building, the boys are working themselves into a frenzy. The dance becomes something menacing as 'out of the terror rose another desire, thick, urgent, blind – the desire to kill'. Once again, Golding uses language to highlight the brutality of the event. The list of adjectives suggests the depth of their depravity and also suggests the speed at which they are acting. Into the midst of this stumbles the innocent Simon. He is the only one who can see that the fear of the beast is irrational and that the ones that they really have to fear are themselves. At first, Golding refers to him as a thing, which suggests that they don't know it is Simon. However, he then says that 'Simon was crying out', which suggests that they do know that it is him. As they continue to dance, they 'screamed, struck, bit, tore. There were no words, and no movements but the tearing of teeth and claws.'

Uses correct grammatical terminology, which helps develop the analysis.

Analysis of Golding's techniques is excellent.

Good language analysis.

Golding's choice of the animalistic word 'claws' emphasizes the violence and inhumanity of their actions. These are little boys who are now brutally murdering one of their own in a way which can only be described as savage and animalistic. The tribal nature of the dance is indicative of the move that has been made from civilization towards savagery – these boys used to be members of a church choir. The climactic moment, the killing of Simon, is accompanied by violent thunderclaps and flashes of lightning which add to the feeling of fear and hysteria. Once the deed is done, calm returns to the island, but the violence which they once only used on animals has now been used on humans and there is no turning back.

Focuses closely on language.

Considers the wider themes of the novel.

This is a well-written answer. There is some excellent analysis of the language and techniques used by Golding, although this could have been developed more fully.

Sample answer 3

This is an extract from a sample answer from a **Foundation Tier** student, together with examiner comments, to the following question on the novel:

> Look at the extract in Chapter 11 which begins 'Now the painted group felt the otherness of Samneric' and ends 'Ralph's lips formed a word but no sound came.'
>
> What do you think makes this a tense moment in the novel?
> You should consider:
> - what happens
> - how the different boys react
> - the words and phrases Golding uses.

Needs to be developed more fully.

This part of the novel is tense because it is when Piggy gets killed. He, Ralph and Samneric have gone to see Jack to try to get Piggy's glasses back and Piggy can't see what is happening, which puts him in a position of weakness.

Needs to be explained more clearly.

At the beginning of the extract, it says that 'Jack was inspired'. This shows that he hadn't really decided what to do until now. He is making things up as he goes along which means that he hasn't thought about the consequences. This might make him more dangerous.

Quotation provides support.

This is too colloquial for an essay.

'[T]he painted group' makes the extract tense because we know that the masks make them behave differently. This makes the reader feel that something bad is likely to happen. Jack is obviously angry because he 'spoke between his teeth' and he is trying to show Ralph who's boss. This makes things tense because we know that the thing he most wants is power.

Needs analysis of the language in the quotation.

When Ralph swears at Jack, 'You're a beast and a swine and a bloody, bloody thief', this shows how tense things are. Until now, Ralph has always been in control of how he behaves and this shows that he has lost control. This makes the reader feel as though he might beat Jack when he charged because we have never seen him behave like this before.

Links helpfully to other parts of the text.

When they are fighting, it is tense because we don't know who is going to win. They are both 'panting and furious' while the other boys cheer behind them. This reminds the reader of the cheering on the beach and makes it tense in case something like that happens again. This shows that the pack mentality exists

However, the conch is soon a source of conflict when Jack declares that "The conch doesn't count on top of the mountain". This shows that Jack is already beginning to rebel against the rules and Ralph's authority and foreshadows later events. This forces Ralph to assert his authority: "Where the conch is, that's a meeting. The same up here as down there." Although Jack publicly agrees with him, the reader understands that there is already a difference in opinion about the conch, but also about the rules. This creates a sense of unease.

Uses appropriate terminology and sets up the idea of the conch being a symbol for rules rather than just an object.

Reader response considered.

Gradually, the boys start to show less respect for the conch. When Jack and others leave the assembly, Piggy wants Ralph to call them back, but Ralph says "If I blow the conch and they don't come back; then we've had it". This shows that Ralph realizes that the power of the conch is diminishing, while Piggy still has faith in it. At the end of Chapter 10, when the tribe sneak into the camp and take Piggy's glasses, he misunderstands what they have come for and is surprised that "They didn't come for the conch". The power of the conch as a symbol of authority is gone, but Piggy's belief in civilization remains. He does not understand that while Ralph's power lay in personality, Jack's will lie in practical things and he has no need for the conch.

Insightful analysis of the quotation.

The end of the conch marks the end of civilization on the island. The fact that Piggy and Ralph take the conch to Jack's part of the island shows that they are clinging to the hope that civilization can be returned. Jack's tribe, however, are no longer interested in the old ways: they have created a new type of life for themselves. Piggy dies believing in civilization and the power of the conch: 'The rock struck Piggy a glancing blow from chin to knee; the conch exploded into a thousand white fragments and ceased to exist.' As he dies, the last chance for civilization to be returned to the island is smashed to pieces, like the conch.

The conch was a symbol of power and leadership, of civilization and the world the boys left behind. It was also a symbol of the link between Ralph and a 'true, wise friend'. With the conch, Golding shows us the importance of remaining civilized and what the consequences of not having rules can be.

Makes a good concluding summary.

This answer shows a confident response to the text. It includes plenty of evidence and there is some analysis of language and reference to context. The wider significance of the conch is well considered. It could be improved with a closer focus on language.

Glossary

Adonis-like like a god

allegory a story with a hidden meaning in which characters, events and objects have a symbolic function

Allies the countries, including Britain, France and the United States, which combined forces to fight Nazi Germany

anarchy lawlessness

archaic old-fashioned

civilians the ordinary people who were not fighting in the war

climax a high point; the most dramatic moment in a novel or play

colloquial informal, everyday speech

connotation an implied meaning, such as ideas or qualities suggested by a word

democracy a system where everyone gets to vote for the leader and have a say in the way the country is run

democratic a type of government which promotes social equality

deus ex machina a plot device used to resolve a problem in the nick of time

dictator a person who has gained power by force and who has total power over a country

dictatorship a system where the leader makes all of the decisions themselves; a dictator usually takes power by force and has not been elected

dystopian extremely negative; a dystopia is an imaginary place where everything is bad

empire a group of countries spread over a large area which is ruled by one person (e.g. Queen Victoria)

foil a contrasting character used to show up particular qualities in another character

foreboding a feeling that something bad is going to happen

foreshadow hints at future events

free indirect speech where a character's words or thoughts are conveyed directly, but without using speech marks or 'he/she said'

idiolect the individual speech patterns of a person

imagery descriptive language which builds up an image in the reader's mind, e.g. similes and metaphors

imperative verb command verbs, e.g. 'Do our dance'

inhibitions the subconscious rules by which the boys previously lived

ironic using irony; having the opposite effect to what was intended

irrational without reason or logic

juxtaposition two opposite ideas placed side by side to emphasize the link or the difference between them

martyr someone who dies for their beliefs, normally religious

megalomaniac a person obsessed with power

metaphor a comparison of one thing to another to make a description more vivid; a metaphor states that one thing *is* another

omniscient narrator a narrator who knows everything about the characters, including their inner thoughts and motivations

order a state in which rules established to control the behaviour of a community are obeyed

pathetic fallacy where something (like the building storm) reflects the mood in a text

personification a type of metaphor where human qualities are given to objects or ideas

perspective point of view

pessimistic naturally negative

regime a system of government

simile a comparison of one thing to another to make a description move vivid, using the words 'like' or 'as'

Standard English the form of English that is considered the norm and is typically used in formal situations

symbolic using something to represent a concept, idea or theme in a novel

third person from the perspective of a character or voice outside the story, using the pronouns 'he' or 'she'

usurp to take power illegally, often using force

Great Clarendon Street, Oxford OX2 6DP

Oxford University Press is a department of the University of Oxford.
It furthers the University's objective of excellence in research,
scholarship, and education by publishing worldwide in

Oxford   New York

Auckland   Cape Town   Dar es Salaam   Hong Kong   Karachi
Kuala Lumpur   Madrid   Melbourne   Mexico City   Nairobi
New Delhi   Shanghai   Taipei   Toronto

With offices in

Argentina   Austria   Brazil   Chile   Czech Republic   France   Greece
Guatemala   Hungary   Italy   Japan   Poland   Portugal   Singapore
South Korea   Switzerland   Thailand   Turkey   Ukraine   Vietnam

Oxford is a registered trade mark of Oxford University Press
in the UK and in certain other countries

British Library Cataloguing in Publication Data

Data available

ISBN 978-0-19-839043-5

10 9 8 7 6 5 4 3 2

Printed in China by Printplus

Acknowledgements
The publisher and author are grateful for permission to reprint the following copyright material:

Extracts from *Lord of the Flies* by William Golding (Faber & Faber, 1997) and from *The Hot Gates* (Faber & Faber,
1965), reprinted by permission of the publishers.

Cover: Penny Tweedie/Alamy; **p6:** Pictorial Press Ltd/Alamy; **p9:** AF archive/Alamy; **p12:** The Moviestore
Collection Ltd; **p16:** AF archive/Alamy; **p20:** AF archive/Alamy; **p22:** Moviestore collection Ltd/Alamy; **p24:**
AF archive/Alamy; **p28:** photogerson/Shutterstock; **p30:** Bettmann/CORBIS; **p31:** Corbis; **p34:** Trinity Mirror/
Mirrorpix/Alamy; **p38:** AF archive/Alamy; **p41:** United Archives GmbH/Alamy; **p45:** Moviestore Collection/Rex
Features; **p48:** Moviestore collection Ltd/Alamy; **p50:** Lord of the Flies 1963, Two Arts/CD/The Kobal Collection;
p56: AF archive/Alamy; **p58:** Eky Studio/Shutterstock; **p61:** leonid_tit/Shutterstock; **p62:** Pictorial Press Ltd/
Alamy; **p64:** JeninVA/Shutterstock; **p66:** AF archive/Alamy; **p70:** Robbie Jack/Corbis; **p73:** Robbie Jack/Corbis

Map artwork by Barking Dog Art.